MUSICIANS INSTITUTE™

MASTER CLASS

PROGRESSIVE ROCK BASS

T0085044

A Guide to Developing Creative Concepts and Techniques

by Christopher Maloney

Interior Photos by Kristina Balobeck

ISBN 978-1-4234-8091-4

HAL•LEONARD® CORPORATION

7777 W. BLUEMOUND RD. P.O. BOX 13819 MILWAUKEE, WI 53213

In Australia Contact:
Hal Leonard Australia Pty. Ltd.
4 Lentara Court
Cheltenham, Victoria, 3192 Australia
Email: ausadmin@halleonard.com.au

Visit Hal Leonard Online at
www.halleonard.com

Contents

1 Introduction: Confessions of a Progressive Rock Bassist

Having been trained to be a professional bassist, I have attempted to avoid labels my whole career. In many ways, being a true professional musician requires you to be a chameleon of sorts, to have the ability to play through any number of styles and any number of musical situations. If someone thinks of you as a jazz bassist, then you won't necessarily get a call to do a pop recording session. If someone thinks of you as a metal player, you won't get referred to do the R&B gig that you'd love. Thus, I never wanted to be labeled anything except as a "professional bassist." As I eventually also became a singer/songwriter, I was happy to just call myself a "professional musician" and avoid the misconceptions and stereotypes that labels inevitably bring.

However, being a progressive *player* (not to mention a progressive person) means to have the ability to move things forward and stretch the music you are playing into new directions. Where would we be without progress, right? The *Encarta World English Dictionary* in my computer tells me that *progress* means, "the gradual development or improvement of something." Sounds pretty good, I think. If people can think of you as being a musician who can bring about improvement in their music, that's pretty cool! Call yourself a "progressive bassist" if you must.

In order to be a progressive player, you need to have skills that will allow you to try different things musically. It could be that your skill is that you have a wild imagination. Your skill could be shoving convention to the side and experimenting with sounds, tones, technique, and different scales. At the same time, to be really effective as a progressive player, you should have some solid skills under your fingertips. You should have a strong knowledge of useful scales, different kinds of technique, and a handle on different types of grooves and timing. These are the kinds of things I will focus on in this book.

What Is Progressive Rock?

So why progressive rock? What is progressive rock anyway? Let's go back to my little computer dictionary. Yes, the term *progressive rock* is actually in the *Encarta World English Dictionary* in my computer (who knew?). These folks define it as "a type of rock music originating in the early 1970s and characterized by technically elaborate and sometimes experimental arrangements." I like that definition a lot. It doesn't name any bands or any players, and it's vague enough for you to fill in the blanks as far as what "elaborate" or "experimental" means. These are descriptive terms that mean different things to different people. To some, the Beatles could be a progressive rock band because their later music was more experimental than the pop music of the day. To others, the band Cream could be progressive because their blues arrangements were more elaborate than the songs in that style. Of course, these bands were formed in the sixties, but does that make them any less progressive?

So there's the label and style of progressive rock and the *concept* of playing rock progressively. The latter is what we'll focus on in this book. In the next chapter, we'll talk about the genre, style, and label of progressive rock. This means we'll check out the bands that started the prog rock era, the different sub-genres of progressive rock and the bands and players today that are keeping that style alive. However, I would very much like you to not think of progressive rock in terms of just bands or even styles. Think of progressive rock in terms of a concept; the ability to move rock music forward from its typical form, style,

5

and arrangements—that's what this book is all about. We're going to be studying the knowledge and techniques that many of prog players used to create their imaginative and groundbreaking music. I don't want you to play like a progressive rock bassist, I want you to *be* a progressive rock bassist.

How This Book Works

Each chapter contains what I think is a very important musical concept that all bass players should learn, but is also essential for someone who wants to be a progressive rock bassist. The musical examples will be written in standard bass clef notation and tablature. In some instances, I'll have some neck diagrams as well to help you see the way certain scales are laid out across the neck. After each concept is introduced and discussed, I'll have several sample basslines written out for you to play. For many examples, there will be a corresponding CD track to listen to.

Musical Examples

You will notice that all the musical examples (with one or two exceptions) are based on either an A or D scale. The roots of these scales and basslines are on the fifth fret of the E string (A) or the fifth fret of the A string (D). This was done intentionally for a couple of reasons: first, it's easier to notice the slight differences in scales both visually and aurally by playing them in the same area of the neck and on the same roots. Second, these are roots that are used a lot in rock music. Once you learn each scale and bassline in the written key, you should try to play it on different roots and in different parts of the neck.

CD Info

The examples on the CD are played with a classic power trio—guitar, bass, and drums. Although much of progressive music incorporates keyboards, it was decided to not have keyboards on these recorded examples. The main reason for this is that it is much easier to hear what the bass is playing, and therefore, easier for you to play along with the recordings with as little instrumentation as possible.

Bass—Christopher Maloney
Guitar—Jeff Kollman
Drums—Shane Gaalaas

The three musicians above have played together under the name of Cosmosquad. If you enjoy the examples, check out the group's live DVD *Lights...Camera...SQUAD!* available from Marmaduke/Sunset Records at *www.cosmosquad.com*. This band has also played on Christopher Maloney's solo CDs, which you can check out at *www.christophermaloney.com*. Yes, these are shameless plugs. Get into it!

Recorded at Crumb Studios West, Simi Valley, California, U.S.A. Engineered by Shane Gaalaas. Produced by James Halstead and Christopher Maloney. All music written by Christopher Maloney.

Chapter 1

Practice Tips

For the concepts and examples of each chapter, try to use the following methods and tips to help you learn this material more quickly and efficiently:

Read: Please read through the text to get the ideas and concepts from a mental and intellectual place before you go through the musical examples. It'll be easier for you to get the musical ideas under your fingers this way. Also, I'll be giving helpful hints along the way, so you don't want to miss anything by not reading the text.

Listen: I have recorded many examples for you to listen to. I think this is the easiest way to understand and be able to play new ideas. This will be especially helpful for those of you who have trouble reading the written musical examples.

Practice Slowly: Play along with the recordings to make sure you are playing the idea correctly. You can always listen to the example, stop the recording to get the shapes under your fingers, then go back to the recording and play along. The important thing for you to do is to practice each and every concept and example *very slowly*! You can get the example perfect, and then work it up to speed at your own pace.

I hope that you thoroughly enjoy working through this book. If you are able to really understand and execute the material presented here, you should have little trouble handling the sometimes intricate and complex music of progressive rock. Good luck, work hard, and have fun!!

Christopher Maloney

2 Progressive Rock

This book is not intended to be a "history" book on the style of progressive rock. There are lots of great sources to get this information, including the *Gibraltar Encyclopedia of Progressive Rock* (*www.gepr.net*) and *Prog Archives* (*www.progarchives.com*). However, some background information about the origin of the style, the influential bands and players, and information on the different subgenres of the style is important.

A Brief History of Progressive Rock

As the world passed from the 1960s into the 1970s, it seemed that so many things had changed. Music, more specifically rock music, went through a great deal of change and growth. Gone were the simple chord progressions, straightforward lyrics, and simple arrangements. One can point to the creative arc of the music of the Beatles, *the* most influential rock band of that decade, to see how the genre had changed. Arguably, one could point to *Sgt. Pepper's Lonely Hearts Club Band* as the first "concept album," a term that would come to help define certain aspects of prog rock in the next decade (although the Mothers of Invention album, *Freak Out,* came out a year earlier). Regardless of that, popular music was no longer necessarily a musical style played by ruffians, hooligans, and musically uneducated players. Rock was now a respected musical art form (as well as a multi-million dollar industry) and it was about to make a quantum leap forward in terms of musical sophistication in the 1970s. It was going to get louder, it was going to get darker, it was going to get more complex and more experimental. The time was ripe to push the boundaries of what a rock band could write and play. Rock 'n' roll was ready to progress!

Many musicians wanted to keep the energy and power of electronic instruments in rock music, but they also wanted to push the boundaries of conventional rock arrangements, song lengths, use of meter, as well as harmony and lyrical content. They looked to their more "respected" and "virtuosic" musical brethren in jazz and orchestral music for inspiration. These players were more likely to pull from the influences of Stravinsky, Debussy, Bartok, Varese, John Coltrane, and Miles Davis than from Elvis, Buddy Holly, or even the Beatles. Songs became longer—sometimes exceeding twenty minutes—and taking up an entire side of an LP record. Lyrics started dealing with a wide variety of esoteric topics, including spiritual, medieval, political, and science fiction themes. Simple chord progressions were replaced by the use of extended chords more often found in jazz and twentieth century orchestral compositions. As the player's virtuosity grew, the music became more improvised with lengthy solos mixed with complex unison lines. The dance grooves of 4/4 meter, so essential in early pop and rock music, were intermingled with various other time signatures to add yet another layer of depth. Live performances evolved into elaborate, multi-media events, including lasers, film projection, large stage props, intricate lighting, and even performance art.

There is some debate as to when the prog rock movement began. It could be, as mentioned earlier, with the release of *Sgt. Pepper* in 1967, or perhaps with King Crimson's *Court of the Crimson King* in 1969, or even the Mothers of Invention's *Freak Out* in 1966 (which, in part, inspired *Sgt. Pepper*). There is little debate however, to when the heyday of prog rock ended. It was in 1976 with the release of the Sex Pistols' *Never Mind the Bollocks, Here's the Sex Pistols*. At this time in England, the main epicenter of the prog rock movement, the country was going through very difficult financial and political times. The younger teenagers couldn't relate to the fanciful lyrics and heady music that their older siblings enjoyed. These were angry and disenchanted kids who knew nothing of the flower power, peace signs, and the "tune-in, turn-on, drop-out" philosophy of the late sixties. They were tired of what they considered the pomposity and grandiosity of prog rock music, being played by, as they called them, "boring old farts." They wanted their music simple, fast, and loud. Punk music swept through both England and America (with bands like the Ramones and the Stooges) like a wildfire, and the prog rock movement quickly started to fall out of favor. Not until 1991, with the advent of grunge music (where once again the disenchanted music of youth took over), would rock music see another stylistic purging.

Prog rock changed quite a bit in the 1980s. A new subgenre called "neo-progressive" was developed that was more concise and listener-friendly than the prog music of the seventies. Bands like King Crimson, Genesis, and Yes evolved more of a pop sound while still retaining some of their experimental and expansive writing. Even Frank Zappa and Pink Floyd scored Top 40 hits with the tongue-in-cheek "Valley Girl" and the disco-influenced "Another Brick in the Wall (Part II)," respectively. New bands like Marillion, and even early Metallica, would emerge during this time to keep pushing the boundaries of rock music. Today, there are so many bands that keep expanding the idea of what rock music is that it's hard to put just the progressive rock label on them. Some, like Dream Theater, Spock's Beard, and Porcupine Tree, are more easily identifiable as derivative of progressive rock, while bands like Tool, Phish, Meshuggah, the Mars Volta, and the White Stripes continue to establish new genres of rock music.

Bands and Subgenres

Of course, we can talk about progressive rock all day, but one has to hear it in its many forms and subgenres to start to grasp the music. Below you will find a very simplistic list of prog rock genres and bands that can get you started with understanding and appreciating this exciting style of music.

Suggested Listening

This genre being "progressive" rock, most bands incorporate elements of many of the listed subgenres.

Classical/Symphonic: King Crimson, Yes, Genesis; Emerson, Lake & Palmer; Gentle Giant, and Spock's Beard.

Hard Rock: Rush, Deep Purple, Iron Maiden, Kansas, Jethro Tull, Dream Theater, Fates Warning, Porcupine Tree, and Marillion.

Fusion: Brand X, Weather Report, Mahavishnu Orchestra, Return to Forever, Soft Machine, and Gong.

Space Rock: Pink Floyd, David Bowie, Ozric Tentacles, and the Mars Volta.

Experimental: Frank Zappa, Captain Beefheart, and Primus.

Progressive Rock Bassists

It is very important as well to not only know the bands, but to know who's actually playing bass. Make sure you learn a little something about some of these fine players. Some of these bands have had numerous bassists, in which case only one or two principal players are listed.

King Crimson—Tony Levin, Greg Lake, John Wetton
Yes—Chris Squire
Genesis—Mike Rutherford
Emerson, Lake & Palmer—Greg Lake
Gentle Giant—Ray Shulman
Spock's Beard—Dave Meros
Rush—Geddy Lee
Deep Purple—Roger Glover, Glenn Hughes
Iron Maiden—Steve Harris
Kansas—Rod Mikinski, Billy Greer
Jethro Tull—Jeffrey Hammond, Dave Pegg
Dream Theater—John Myung
Fates Warning—Joe DiBiase, Joey Vera
Porcupine Tree—Colin Edwin
Marillion—Diz Minnitt, Pete Trewavas
Brand X—Percy Jones
Weather Report—Jaco Pastorius
Mahavishnu Orchestra—Rick Laird, Ralphe Armstrong
Return to Forever—Stanley Clarke
Soft Machine—Kevin Ayers, Hugh Hopper
Gong—Mike Howlett
Pink Floyd—Roger Waters
David Bowie—Trevor Bolder
Ozric Tentacles—Vinny Shillito
The Mars Volta—Juan Alderete
Frank Zappa—Arthur Barrow, Patrick O'Hearn, Tom Fowler, Scott Thunes
Captain Beefheart—Jerry Handley, Mark Boston
Primus—Les Claypool

Skills of the Progressive Rock Bassist

As stated briefly in chapter one, a bass player who is looking to play in a progressive rock band needs to have many skills to call upon. One has to be well-versed in many styles, all keys, different meters, and various techniques in order to handle the demands of this kind of music. Each bassist listed above has his own strengths and weaknesses when it comes to playing bass. The element that binds these players together however, has nothing to do with playing bass. It has to do with having a command of the "rules" of music and a complete disregard for following those rules. A player with all the necessary skills to play this style could be any number of qualified session musicians. To be a true progressive rock bassist, you need to have more than that. You need to be able to use your skills in a creative and unconventional way. All of the things you will learn in this book will certainly make you a very solid bass player. Make sure that you take the information presented here and truly make it your own, and you will become a progressive rock bass player!

3 Fret-Hand Technique Exercises

For playing most styles of music, proper technique is very important. For playing progressive rock, it is absolutely essential. The demands of playing such challenging music, which encompasses many different styles, scales, grooves, and meter, require you to play the notes with pinpoint accuracy. You will not be able to rise to this challenge if you have poor technique.

Just a little bit of preliminary information first: the fret hand is the hand that gets to play all the notes on the bass. We play these notes by putting one finger in between two frets (those metal things on your neck, silly!), pushing the string down onto the neck, and plucking that string with our other hand (plucking hand).

For these exercises, please pluck the strings with your fingers on your right hand (for right handers). If you are primarily a pick or slap player, this will really help you improve your finger technique. Remember, if you are going to play the challenging music of progressive rock, you need to have a good grip on all the available techniques. You can then determine what technique to use based on what's right for the specific song, and not from some deficiency in your playing. *Make sure you always alternate your index and middle fingers.*

The exercises in this chapter may seem rudimental to some of you, but they are absolutely essential for building the muscular dexterity needed to play challenging basslines. Once you have a handle on the following exercises, you should play them for 5–10 minutes a day as your daily warm up. It's a great way to keep your hands in shape.

Exercise 1: One Finger Per Fret

Start by placing your first finger (index finger) of your fret hand on the fifth fret, E string, as shown in the photo.

Now, push the string down to the neck at fret 5 using your first finger, and pluck the string with your other hand. You should be able to hear the note clearly. If not, push down a little harder or move your finger more to the middle of the fret.

Now, while still holding down your index finger, put your middle finger down on the next fret and pluck the string. Follow this by putting down your ring finger on the next fret and pluck the string. Finally, put your pinky down on the next fret and pluck the string once again. Each finger is playing its own fret. Remember: one finger per fret.

Again, this may seem remedial to some players, but proper technique is essential in order to play challenging bass lines. This exercise helps get your fret-hand technique solid!

Take a look at the figures below to see the proper way to play this exercise.

You should have heard four totally different notes. If not, go back and try this again.

At this point, you should do the same exercise starting on the fifth fret of the other strings (A, D, and G). Start with your index finger and work your way up the frets slowly. After you finish playing the G string, you should work your way down the strings staying at the same fret. Where before you played E, A, D, G, now start over and play G, D, A, E. You can repeat this cycle as much as you want.

Read through the musical example below. This shows you the notes you need to play on the strings you need to play them on. After you play through the exercise a few times, you should have it pretty well memorized. Just remember to play all strings ascending and descending.

Example 1: One Finger Per Fret

Track 1

It's *really* important now for you to put the CD in and listen to the above exercise. This way, you can really hear what the notes sound like and make sure you are playing this correctly.

What to Do/What Not to Do

When you practice this exercise, make sure that you keep in mind the following:

1. Make sure you have a clear-sounding note—no fret buzz.
2. Make sure you play on your fingertips.
3. Make sure you keep your knuckles curved. Don't "break" the knuckle closest to your fingertip.
4. Make sure you are alternating the index and middle fingers of your plucking hand. Don't be a "one-fingered wonder".
5. Make sure you are always sustaining a note. Don't allow any silence between your notes.
6. Play this exercise *very slowly*—this is not a speed exercise. Do it as slowly as you can to play it with accuracy.
7. **Bonus**: Keep all of your fingers down on the neck and move only the finger you are playing—*even when you change strings*. This is pretty tough to do initially, as your hands will get quite a stretch. However, it'll get easier in time and will give you strong fret-hand technique to handle those tricky progressive rock basslines.

This exercise is *extremely important*. Practiced properly, it will give you the skill, strength, coordination, independence, and stamina to play any style of music. Over time, you can shift this exercise from something you focus intently on everyday to something you use as a good warm-up drill to quickly limber up your fret hand before any rehearsals or gigs.

Exercise 2: Finger Gymnastics

Here is where we get our fingers really nimble. You are going to employ the same one-finger-per-fret technique we learned above and apply it to the following exercises. Try these examples where you will be crossing strings. This is very challenging to play accurately and in time, so start out very slowly. This will help you gain finger independence and strength, which is necessary in playing the sometimes demanding basslines of progressive rock.

Example 2: One String Crossing

Example 3: Two String Crossing

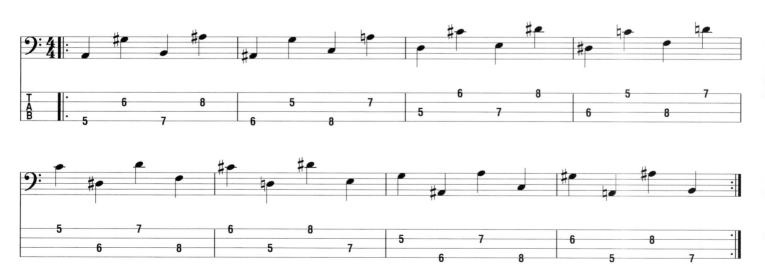

You can also play different rhythms with your plucking hand. The example below is the same string-crossing Exercise 2. In this case, we are playing each note twice in an eighth-note rhythm.

Example 4: Adding Rhythms to Exercise 2

Try different rhythmic subdivisions (i.e., eighth notes, triplets, sixteenth notes, etc.) to engage your plucking hand in this exercise. This will help you build speed and endurance in that hand.

Sample Basslines

You can actually turn this atonal finger exercise into some cool bassline ideas. Check out the sample basslines below, and you can see how you can create some music out of a simple exercise. Try to create your own basslines.

Example 5: Sample Bassline from Exercise 2

Example 6: Sample Bassline from Exercise 3

Assignment

1. Practice the One-Finger-Per-Fret exercise everyday for at least 15 minutes. You can do it for longer if you wish. Be sure that you are doing the exercise properly by following the section What to Do/What Not to Do.
2. Try your hand at some of the Finger Gymnastic exercises. You can do one or two of these a day if you wish. As your fingers get more coordinated, try increasing the speed.
3. Play through some of the sample basslines.

Rock Basics: Major Pentatonics

There are dozens of scales that are very useful in playing music. However, for all the styles and subgenres of rock, the most widely used scales are called *pentatonic scales*. In fact, of all the styles of music I play as a freelance bassist (rock, pop, jazz, fusion, funk, country, latin, and acoustic/folk), these are the scales I use 90 percent of the time. It doesn't mean that the pentatonic scales are the only ones you should learn, but they are certainly an essential part of the rock basics.

Note: If you already have a working knowledge of these scales, you may want to skip to the sample basslines section of this chapter. I would suggest stopping by and checking out the extended fingering patterns however. I find that most bassists don't have a really good handle on this pattern. You should, because it's the one with the most vibe!

Penta-what???

As the name implies, the *pentatonic scale* has five notes in it ("penta" means five). There is a *major pentatonic scale* and a *minor pentatonic scale*. The major pentatonic scale uses five notes from the major scale, and the minor pentatonic scale uses five notes from the minor scale. For this chapter, we will look at the major pentatonic scale.

The major pentatonic scale uses the 1st, 2nd, 3rd, 5th, and 6th notes from the major scale. You will also see the octave note in the following patterns, but that is the same as the first note. The 4th and 7th notes of the major scale are not used in the pentatonic scale.

Layout of the Two Basic Major Pentatonic Shapes

Major Scale Starting with the 2nd Finger on the E String (A Major)

Major Pentatonic Scale Starting with the 2nd Finger/E String

Major Scale Starting with the 4th Finger/E String (A Major)

16

Major Pentatonic Scale Starting with the 4th Finger/E String

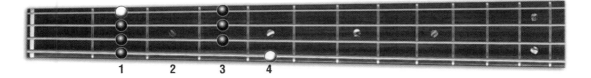

We can also use these shapes with the roots on the A string. We won't see an octave-to-octave shape, but we are seeing more notes below our root.

Major Scale Starting with the 2nd Finger/A String (D Major)

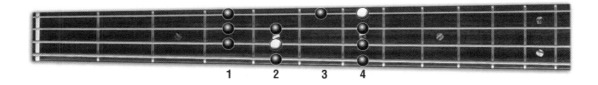

Major Pentatonic Scale Starting with the 2nd Finger/A String

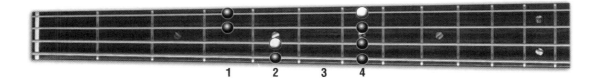

Major Scale Starting with the 4th Finger/A String (D Major)

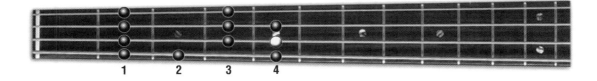

Major Pentatonic Scale Starting with the 4th Finger/A String

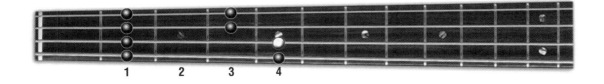

These simple shapes have been used to create some of the most memorable melodies in music. These are *essential* to learn if you want to be a bassist. Why is that? We'll talk about that later. Now, let's check out the "cool" way to play the major pentatonic scale.

Layout of the Two Extended Major Pentatonic Shapes

The fingerings below are different from the simple major pentatonic shapes in one way—we have to shift positions to play these patterns. Why would we learn a fingering pattern that has us moving up the neck instead of staying in one place? Wouldn't it be easier to just keep our fingers in one area of the neck? Perhaps, and in some circumstances, it's better to use the simple shapes we've already learned. However, playing the following extended patterns allows us to utilize certain dynamic playing techniques such as slides, hammer-ons, pull-offs, and bending. These techniques give these scales a more dynamic sound. You'll be able to hear it in the recorded examples.

Even though these fingerings and shapes are different, we are still playing the 1st, 2nd, 3rd, 5th, and 6th notes of the major pentatonic scale.

Extended Major Pentatonic Scale Starting on the E String (A Major)

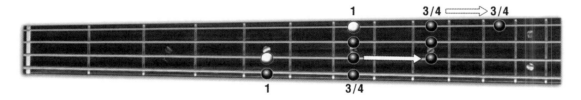

Extended Major Pentatonic Scale Starting on the A String (D Major)

Usage of These Scale Shapes

I mentioned before that these pentatonic shapes are essential for all bassists to learn. This is because you can use these patterns over a wide variety of chords. Remember that, with major pentatonic scales, we omit the 4th and 7th notes of the major scale. This allows us to use the major pentatonic over most major-sounding chords.

Scale	Chords to Use With
Major Pentatonic Scale	Power Chords, Major Triads, Major Sevens, Dominant Sevens

The power chord has an open sound, the major triad has a simple and happy sound, the major seven chord has a pretty sound, and the dominant seven chord has a bluesy sound, yet you can play the same major pentatonic shape over all of these chords. As you can see, it's pretty useful.

Chapter 4

Sample Basslines

Okay, now that we've learned the shapes and the application of this scale, let's start putting it to work. Play the following samples basslines. I'll have you do them with the different shapes that we learned, but you should try to take each line and try it with all the positions (i.e., 2nd finger, 4th finger, extended pattern).

Example 1: Major Pentatonic with 2nd finger

Track 4 — *Play 8 times*

Example 2: Major Pentatonic with 4th finger

Track 5 — *Play 8 times*

Example 3: Major Pentatonic in Extended Pattern

Track 6 — *Play 8 times*

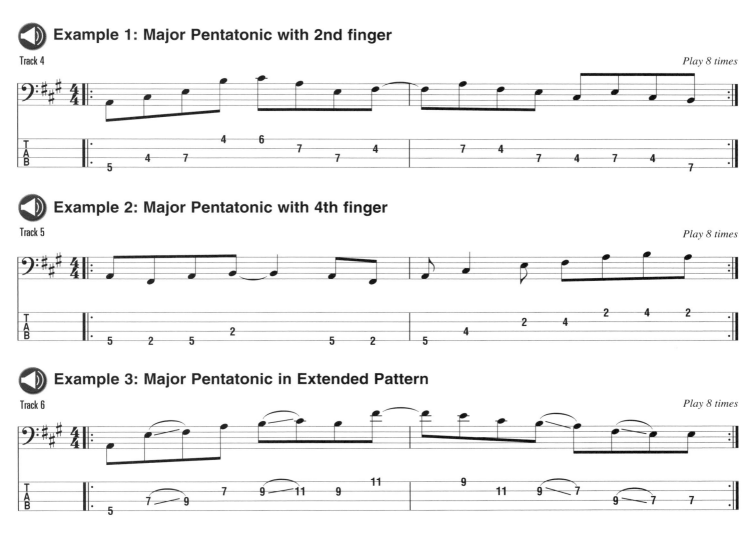

Very cool. Now, we'll check out some lines where we are playing over different chords. For the first example, you can play the A chord with your 2nd finger on the E string and the D chord with your 2nd finger on the A string.

Example 4: Major Pentatonic with Two Chords (2nd finger)

Track 7 — *Play 8 times*

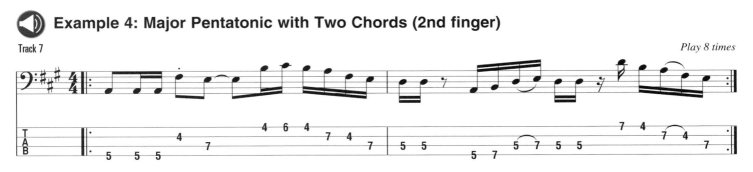

19

Example 5: Major Pentatonic with Two Chords (4th finger)

Track 8

Play 8 times

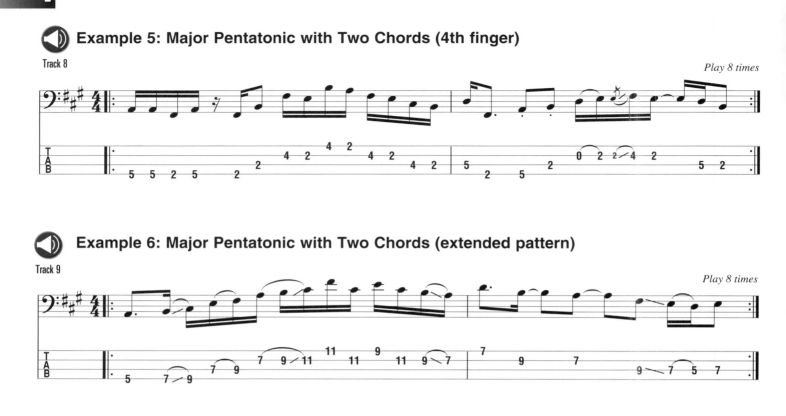

Example 6: Major Pentatonic with Two Chords (extended pattern)

Track 9

Play 8 times

As you can see (and hopefully hear), the major pentatonic scale works over all these chords. If you can *really* get your pentatonic patterns down, then it's relatively easy to learn all your modes. Although we won't go into the topic in much detail here, the below chart shows you how to add a couple of notes to play modes that are more specific to the various chords.

Mode	Add to Pentatonic	Chords to Use With
Ionian (major scale)	4th and 7th	Power Chords, Major Triads, Major Sevens
Lydian	$\sharp$4th and 7th	Power Chords, Major Triads, Major Sevens
Mixolydian	4th and $\flat$7th	Power Chords, Major Triads, Dominant Sevens

Assignment

1. Review the *six* patterns you've learned to play the major pentatonic scale (two on the E string, two on the A string, and the two extended patterns). Play them very slowly and try to commit them to memory as quickly as you can. You will be using these patterns for the rest of your life!
2. Play over the sample lines. These are really important because you don't just want to learn how to play the scales. You also want to hear them being used with various chords and at various tempos. This will also begin or add to your growing vocabulary of basslines.

Rock Basics: Minor Pentatonics

5

Traditionally, the minor pentatonic scale has been *the* most used scale in rock music. Most of your favorite rock riffs use the minor pentatonic or blues scale. We will learn these scales in this chapter. We will also see how to combine the major pentatonic, minor pentatonic, and blues scales to make a hybrid scale that works in many situations.

Let's move straight into learning the shapes of the minor pentatonic scale. The immediate difference between the major and minor pentatonic is that they are based on different scales (major or minor). Another big difference is that scale steps used are different. With the major pentatonic we used the 1st, 2nd, 3rd, 5th, and 6th steps of the major scale, but the minor pentatonic uses the 1st, 3rd, 4th, 5th, and 7th notes of the minor scale. You will also notice a big difference in the sound of each scale. Most people hear the major pentatonic scale as sounding happy, where the minor pentatonic sounds more sad or dark. Obviously, these are subjective descriptions.

Layout of the Two Basic Minor Pentatonic Shapes

Minor Scale Starting with the 1st Finger on the E String (A Minor)

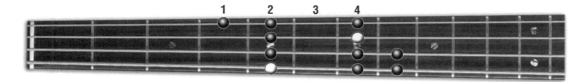

Minor Pentatonic Scale Starting with the 1st Finger/E String

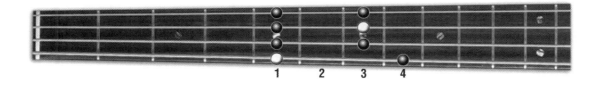

Minor Scale Starting with the 4th Finger/E String (A Minor)

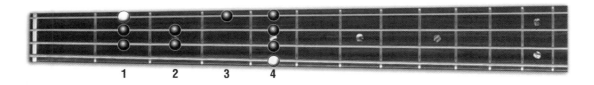

21

The Minor Pentatonic Scale Starting with the 4th Finger/E String

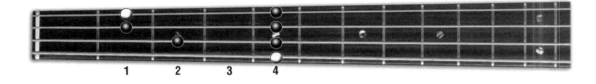

We can also use these shapes with the roots on the A string. As with the major pentatonics, we won't see an octave-to-octave shape, but we are seeing more notes below our root.

Minor Scale Starting with the 1st Finger on the A String (D Minor)

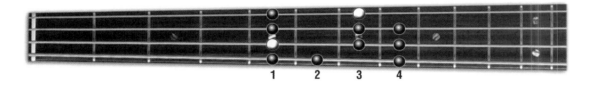

Minor Pentatonic Scale Starting with the 1st Finger/A String

Minor Scale Starting with the 4th Finger/A String (D Minor)

Minor Pentatonic Scale Starting with the 4th Finger/A String

Layout of the Two Extended Minor Pentatonic Shapes

As we did with the extended major pentatonic shapes, we have to shift to play these patterns. Again, these extended shapes allow us to play these scales in a more exciting and dynamic way. The slides, hammer-ons, and other dynamic tools give our basslines more feeling and style.

Even though these fingerings and shapes are different, we are still playing the 1st, 3rd, 4th, 5th, and 7th notes of the minor pentatonic scale.

Extended Minor Pentatonic Scale Starting on the E String (A Minor)

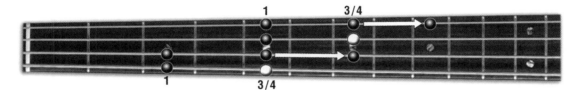

Extended Minor Pentatonic Scale Starting on the A String (D Minor)

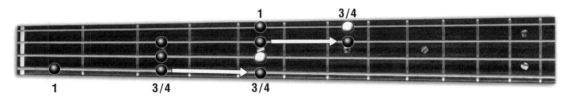

Usage of These Scale Shapes

With the minor pentatonic scales, we omitted the 2nd and 6th notes of the minor scale. This allows us to use the minor pentatonic over most minor-sounding chords.

Scale	Chords to Use With
Minor Pentatonic Scale	Power Chords, Minor Triads, Minor Sevens, Dominant Sevens

You may notice from the above chart that you can play the minor pentatonic scale over a dominant chord. This seems confusing, as the dominant seven chord has a *major* 3rd in it. However, it also has a *minor* 7th. With that, and the fact that our ears are used to over 100 years of blues music that makes the major 3rd of dominant chords sound slightly flat, the minor pentatonic gives you another option to play over.

As with the major pentatonic scales, it's relatively easy to learn all your modes using these scales as a reference. Although we won't go into the topic in much detail here, the below chart shows you how to add a couple of notes to play modes that are more specific to the various chords.

Mode	Add to Pentatonic	Chords to Use With
Aeolian (Minor Scale)	2nd and 6th	Power Chords, Minor Triads, Minor Sevens
Dorian	2nd and Major 6th	Power Chords, Minor Triads, Minor Sevens, Minor Sixes
Phrygian	♭2nd and 6th	Power Chords, Minor Triads, Minor Sevens

Blues Scale

We can add another cool element to the minor pentatonic by adding the note between the 4th and 5th step, called the *flat 5th*. We also call this the "blues note." Adding only this note changes our minor pentatonic scale into the blues scale.

Blues Scale with the 1st Finger on the E String

Blues Scale with Extended Fingering

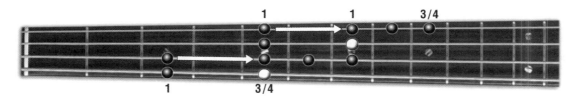

Note: the minor pentatonic shape with the 4th finger is not conducive for playing the blues scale.

Chapter 5

Minor Pentatonic/Blues Scale Sample Basslines

Play the following sample basslines. As with last chapter, play them with the different shapes that you learned, but you should also take each line and try it in all the positions (i.e., 1st finger, 4th finger, extended pattern).

 Example 1: Minor Pentatonic with 1st finger

Track 10

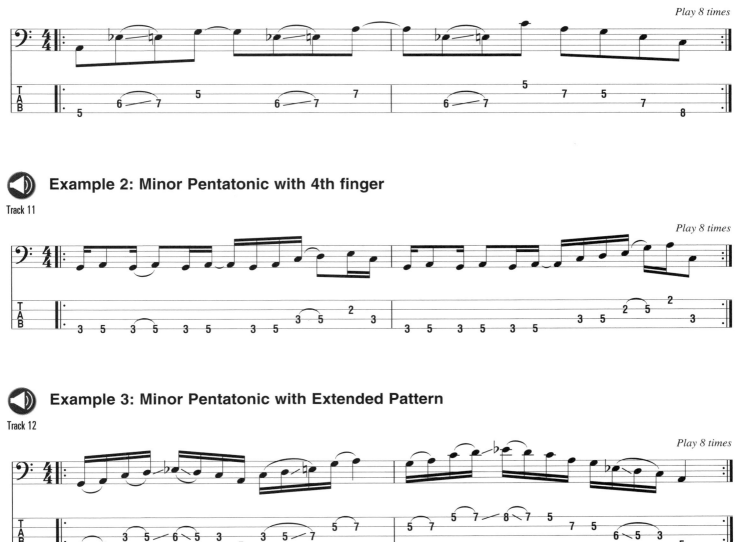

 Example 2: Minor Pentatonic with 4th finger

Track 11

 Example 3: Minor Pentatonic with Extended Pattern

Track 12

Excellent. Now, we'll check out some lines where we are playing over different chords. For the first example, you can play the A chord with your 1st finger on the E string and the D chord with your 1st finger on the A string (or any fingering from the other patterns).

Example 4: Minor Pentatonic with Two Chords (1st finger)

Track 13

Example 5: Minor Pentatonic with Two Chords (4th finger)

Track 14

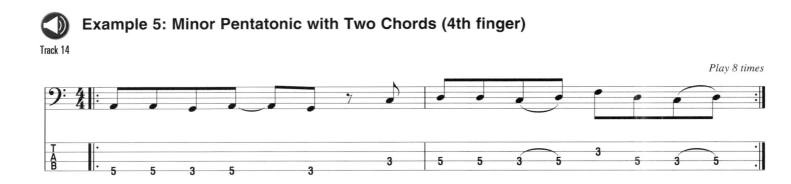

Example 6: Minor Pentatonic with Two Chords (Extended Pattern)

Track 15

Hybrid Pentatonic Scale: Combining Major and Minor Pentatonic/Blues Scales

First of all, I just made up the name "hybrid pentatonic scale." Don't ask anyone if they know of this scale, or they may look at you in a very strange way. However, there really is no name for taking the pentatonic scales and using them all at the same time. If you have a cooler name, just let me know!

Danger:
We would only combine these scales in two instances:
1. If we are playing over a dominant chord. Remember that the major 3rd and minor 7th of this chord gives it both a major and minor sound quality.
2. If there is no overall major or minor tonality, as in playing over a power chord.

Here's what it would look like if you laid out the major pentatonic and minor pentatonic/blues scale out on the neck.

Major and Minor Pentatonic/Blues Starting with 2nd Finger/E String

You may have noticed that we are using almost every note available in the twelve-tone system. That's a pretty crazy collection of notes, and it would be difficult to find a good fingering to use for such a cluttered scale. However, we still can use *all* of these notes if we can organize it better.

Primary Scale: Major Pentatonic

Let's look at the hybrid scale using the major pentatonic as the primary scale. For this, we'll use the 2nd finger pattern.

Major Pentatonic Scale Adding Notes from the Minor Pentatonic with 2nd Finger

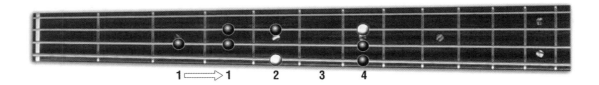

As you can see, it's a lot easier to think of one primary scale, in this case the major pentatonic, and simply add notes from the other scale. In the above diagram, we only added the $\flat$3rd and $\flat$7th from the minor pentatonic scale. This is an easy way to organize these scales to get the most of both pentatonic sounds. You could also add the 4th note of the minor pentatonic and the $\flat$5th from the blues scale.

Let's do the same thing, but play the extended major pentatonic pattern.

Extended Major Pentatonic Pattern Adding Notes from the Minor Pentatonic

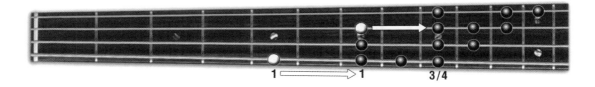

This is a really fun way to make the normally happy major pentatonic scale sound darker, funkier, and cooler. Again, we only add the $\flat$3rd and $\flat$7th, but you can throw in the other notes as well.

Primary Scale: Minor Pentatonic

Now, let's look at this hybrid scale from the minor pentatonic point of view. This works best using the extended fingering. For ease of play, we'll omit the 2nd note of the major pentatonic from this combination. Again, you can add it later.

Minor Pentatonic Scale Adding Notes from the Major Pentatonic

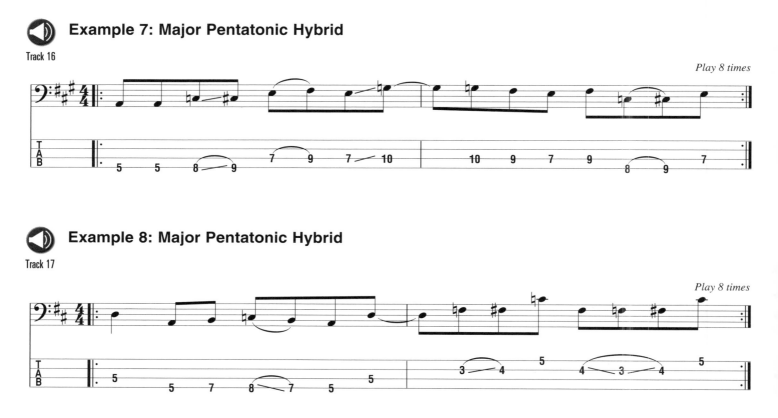

Hybrid Pentatonic Scale Sample Basslines

Here are a couple of basslines with the hybrid scale using the major pentatonic as the primary scale.

Example 7: Major Pentatonic Hybrid

Track 16

Play 8 times

Example 8: Major Pentatonic Hybrid

Track 17

Play 8 times

Here are two basslines with the primary scale being the minor pentatonic/blues scale.

Example 9: Minor Pentatonic Hybrid

Track 18

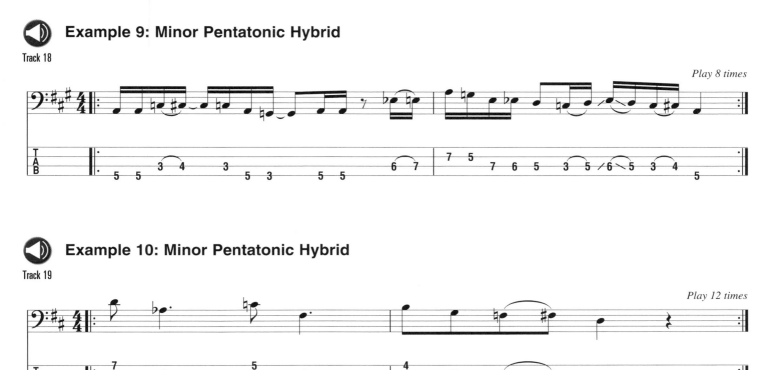

Play 8 times

Example 10: Minor Pentatonic Hybrid

Track 19

Play 12 times

Assignment

1. Review the *six* patterns you've learned to play the minor pentatonic scale (two on the E string, two on the A string, and the two extended patterns). Play them very slowly and try to commit them to memory as quickly as you can. As with the major pentatonic scales, these will be the most important scales you will learn.

2. Play over the sample lines. If it's too fast for you, just play them at your own speed and listen to the CD examples to hear how the line is played and phrased.

6 Alternative Technique: Pick Playing

I always find it funny when people ask me what I play with. "Are you a pick guy? A slapper? Do you play with your fingers?" The answer is: *yes*! It shouldn't be an either/or thing. As a professional player, and certainly a progressive player, you should always use any means at your disposal to play the music you hear in your head. This could mean that you play the bass with a screwdriver if you think it will give you a desired sound.

Do not limit yourself to playing with just one technique. Playing a bassline with a pick gives you a completely different sound than if you play it with your fingers. With practice, you can play some rhythms faster with a pick than your fingers. Why limit yourself to one sound? That would be like a carpenter only using a hammer and never a saw. This carpenter would be pretty limited in what he could build with these restrictions!

Some bassists have an aversion to pick playing because that's what guitarists use. This is a funny rationale. I believe at the heart of every bassist is a modest inferiority complex when it comes to guitarists. Back in the early days of rock, bassists almost always used a pick because they were usually the worst guitarist in the band. Their job as a bassist was pretty much a demotion. Roger Waters, the bassist for Pink Floyd, once said, "I was at one point the lead guitarist, then I was the rhythm guitarist, then I was demoted again to bass. It was a great fear of mine that I would wind up being the drummer!"

Even today, with bass being a much more visible and respected instrument, I find people scoffing at utilizing *anything* a guitarist does. If people see a six-string bass, they'll joke "What are you trying to be? A guitarist!" If people see you playing with a pick, they'll ask mockingly, "You just wish you played guitar." If you plug into any effects box, you'll hear, "Stop trying to be a guitarist!" While this is all funny stuff, don't let it stop you from experimenting with sounds, techniques, tunings, effects, and anything else that helps you create your music.

So, if you already play with a pick, this chapter may be a great opportunity for you to tighten up your technique. If you've never played with a pick or just dabbled with it, this is your chance to open up your sound to a whole new dimension. Of course you're not going to play as well with a pick as you do with your fingers—at least not right away. With practice, you could certainly become more comfortable with the technique and become proficient enough to use it in your bass playing arsenal.

Check out the great bass playing of Chris Squire from Yes and Mike Rutherford from Genesis for some prog rock picking inspiration.

Getting Started

This chapter will focus on exercises to get us comfortable playing with a pick. For many bass players, even choosing a pick will be a daunting task. There are a few things in determining what kind of pick you will use:

Thickness: Picks come in different thicknesses to be used for various playing styles and kinds of strings. Thinner picks are more flexible and tend to offer a wider range of sounds, from soft to loud, while thicker (heavier) picks produce a brighter tone and a more accurate attack. Thus, your decision on thickness will depend on the style of music you play, your gauge of strings, the feel of the pick, and what kind of tone you want.

Pick thickness is usually measured in millimeters. For playing bass, it may be easier to use a thicker pick because of the large size of bass strings. The thickness ranges from Extra Thin/Light (less than .38mm), Light/Thin (.51 to .60mm), Medium (.73 to .81mm), Heavy/Thick (.88 to 1.20mm), to Extra Heavy/Thick (greater than 1.50).

Texture/Material: There are many different materials that can be used to make a pick. The most common are plastic, nylon, tortoise shell (real or imitation), or metal (usually steel). Plastic picks are made from a great variety of materials. Plastic normally gives a balanced overall sound, but they may be prone to breaking. Heavier nylon picks are great because they don't break as easily and they produced a slightly duller tone. Steel picks obviously are not going to break under normally playing situations and will produce a very bright tone.

Flatpick/Thumb-Pick: A lot of bass players (myself included) made the jump to pick playing by using a thumb-pick. The benefit of using this kind of pick is that you can very easily switch from finger to pick playing in the same song. You can use the pick for one part of the tune, then switch to fingers for a more difficult section. After much practice, you'll be able to play everything with a pick and make the choice between a finger or pick-based sound.

Feel: Despite all the other factors and elements, this is *the* most important determination in finding a pick to use. It's got to feel comfortable to play with. Obviously, the technique of playing with a pick will be awkward to beginners at first. At the same time, it should at least feel comfortable in your hands.

Holding the Pick

1. Make an "okay" sign with your plucking hand as seen here, and rest your thumb or index finger gently on top.

2. Slide the non-pointed side of the pick in between your thumb and index finger. Don't hold the pick too tightly.

And there you go. It may feel awkward at first, but this is the proper placement for holding a pick.

You can also try this method:

1. Rest the pick on top of your index finger. Make sure the edge of the pick lines up with the knuckle closest to your fingertip.

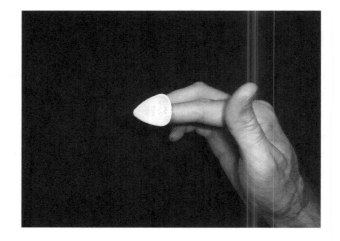

2. Gently place your thumb on top of the pick.

3. Bend your index finger slightly.

Picking Exercises

Now that you know how to hold the pick correctly, let's actually make some noise with it. Let's use our open strings to get started. We will work on two types of picking techniques: *alternate picking* and *downstrokes*.

Alternate Picking: This is where you alternate from a downstroke (where you strum towards the floor) to an upstroke. With practice, you can play very fast using this technique. You do have to be careful however, to make the downstroke and upstroke sound the same.

Downstrokes: This is where you pluck the strings using only downstrokes. You don't strike the string on the up move; you just bring your hand back up to play another downstroke. This technique sounds great when you want to play something very aggressively. However, it's difficult to play things very fast in this way. Obviously, you can play twice as fast using alternate picking, but it doesn't sound as strong that way. Choose your technique based on the sound you want for a particular song.

Example 1: Play this eighth-note example using alternate picking. Then you can try it with only down-strokes. Use your open strings. You can mute the strings you aren't playing by gently resting your fret hand over those strings.

Example 2: Let's play the open strings again, but this time we'll add some interesting rhythms to it. Again, play it with alternate picking and downstrokes.

A really cool effect to use with picking is *fret-hand muting*. This is where you pluck with your picking hand and lay your fretting hand over the strings. The fretting hand mutes the strings to produce a percussive "clicking" sound. This technique is also used with fingerstyle (which you'll see in upcoming Sample Basslines) and slap playing.

Example 3: Play the open E and A strings with the muting technique.

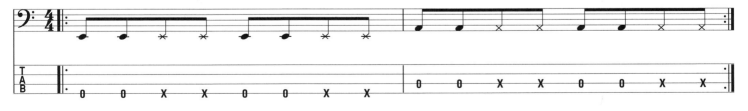

Now let's add some scale work to this technique. We will work with our extended major and minor pentatonic scales.

Example 4: Play the extended major pentatonic scale using both picking techniques.

Track 20

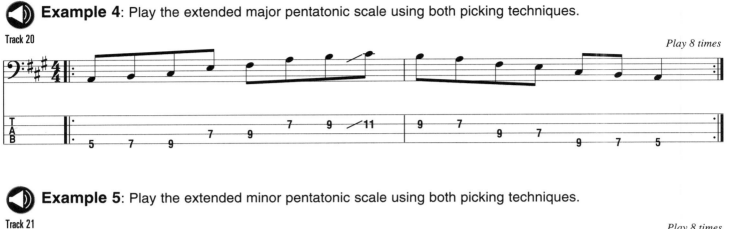

Example 5: Play the extended minor pentatonic scale using both picking techniques.

Track 21

Sample Basslines

Example 6

Track 22

Example 7

Track 23

34

Example 8

Track 24

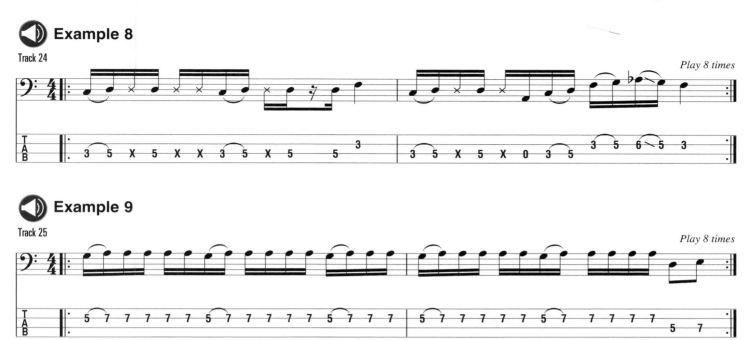

Play 8 times

Example 9

Track 25

Play 8 times

Example 10

Track 26

Play 8 times

Assignment

1. Practice both your alternate and downstroke picking using your open strings as shown in Examples 1, 2, and 3.
2. Practice playing the major and minor pentatonic scales using both picking techniques as shown in Examples 4 and 5.
3. Play through all the sample basslines on your own and with the CD recording. C'mon, you'll love it!

Odd Meter: Playing "4" Keeps

Odd meter, by definition, means "the strange and peculiar space of about 3 feet." No—this is a big lie! Whatever the definition, just the term *odd meter* strikes fear in the hearts of musicians. They can't really describe it; they just know that it's hard to play! This chapter will not only tell you exactly what odd meter is, but demonstrate to you that playing in odd meter is not hard at all. In fact, we will play some phrases that will make odd meter grooves feel pretty natural to you.

What Is Odd Meter?

Think of "meter" as the arrangement of patterns of musical beats. What makes certain patterns "odd" is simply the number of the beats in the pattern. That being said, any rhythmic pattern of odd-numbered beats (i.e., 3, 5, 7, 9, etc.) is considered to be in an odd meter.

Time Signatures: Meters are indicated in the time signature. You may have seen these on a piece of music or heard someone mention, "let's play this in 7/4." Do you know what these numbers mean? Let's check it out.

$\mathbf{4}$—number of beats in a measure
$\mathbf{4}$—the note that gets the beat (in this case, the quarter note)

The top number of the key signature tells you how many beats the measure, or grouping of rhythms, will have in each phrase. For the example above, there are four beats in the measure. When I learned about time signatures in music class as a kid, I could pretty much understand the top number, but the bottom number was confusing to me. Think about the bottom number as a fraction. If you have the bottom number of a fraction as four, you can think of that as a "quarter" of something. Thus, if the bottom number is a four, the quarter note gets the beat. Each measure will have either four quarter notes or a rhythm equivalent to four quarter notes.

This is easy to see in written music. Look at the example below. You can see how there are four beats in each measure, and each beat is represented by a quarter note.

Example 1: Simple 4/4 Measure

We are all familiar with 4/4 time, as it's the most common time found in Western music. It's so common, in fact, that it's sometimes referred to as "common time" and denoted in music with the letter "C" instead of a 4/4 symbol.

Changing the Top Number

By changing the top number of a time signature, you are grouping the rhythms with a different number of beats than 4/4 time. By doing this, you are entering into a whole new world of musical possibilities. It's pretty simple to feel this type of odd meter since the quarter note is still the dominant rhythm. Odd meter grooves in 5/4, 7/4, etc., feel like 4/4 with just a couple of extra beats thrown in.

3/4 Grooves and Sample Basslines

Let's take a look at 3/4 patterns. This time signature is widely used in polkas, waltzes, and some jazz feels. However, it has been known to show its face in many a rock tune.

Example 2

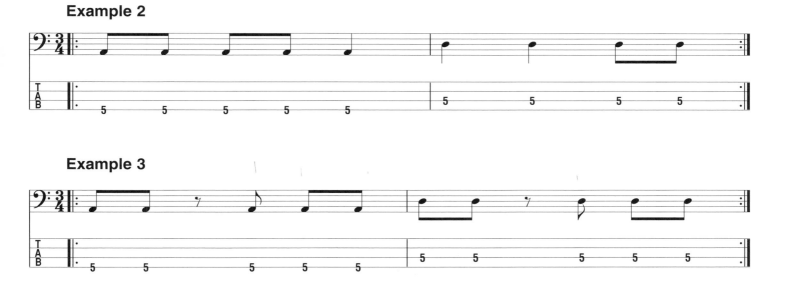

Example 3

We can play another rhythm that will actually feel like a pattern of two. If we play a dotted quarter-note rhythm in the 3/4 measure, we will have two rhythms of equal value. It'll still be 3/4 time, but the pulse will feel like two. You will play on beat one and the "and" of two. This is a great way to "trick" your listener by going from one feel to another. This rhythm will be *very* important for all the other odd-meter grooves.

Example 4

Track 27

Play 16 times

37

Sample 3/4 Basslines

Example 5

Track 28

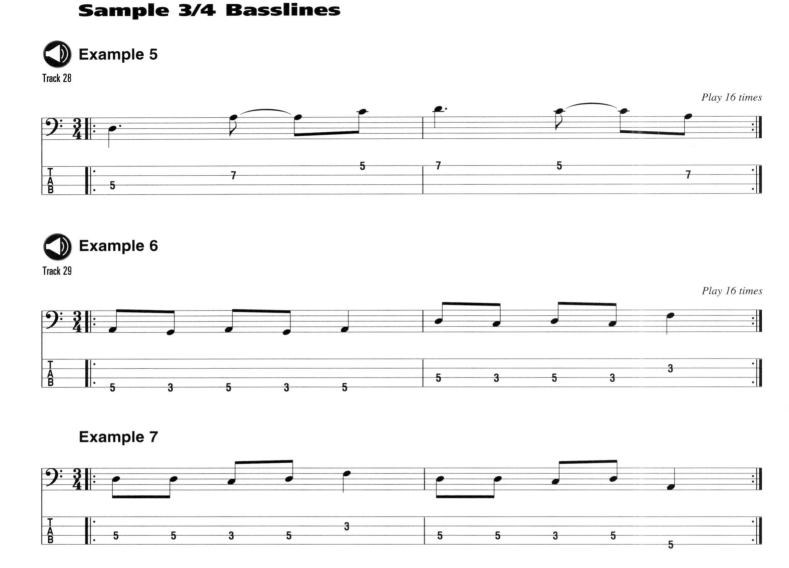

Example 6

Track 29

Example 7

5/4 Grooves and Sample Basslines

Again, this kind of odd meter sort of feels like 4/4 with an extra beat thrown in. It's pretty easy to feel, but you've got to make sure you count!

Example 8

Now, let's try to organize the rhythms to make them easier to feel. We can break down the grouping of 5 into a group of 2 and 3 (2 + 3 = 5!). You can either think of groupings of 5 as a 2/3 or 3/2 pattern. Let's look at a 2/3 pattern.

Example 9

Here, we can bring back our dotted quarter-note rhythm as part of the three grouping.

Example 10

Track 30

Play 8 times

Let's switch the pattern and play a few things with a 3/2 feel.

Example 11

Example 12

Track 31

Play 8 times

Sample 5/4 Basslines

Once again, we are using a combination of major and minor pentatonic scales to create these basslines.

Example 13

Track 32

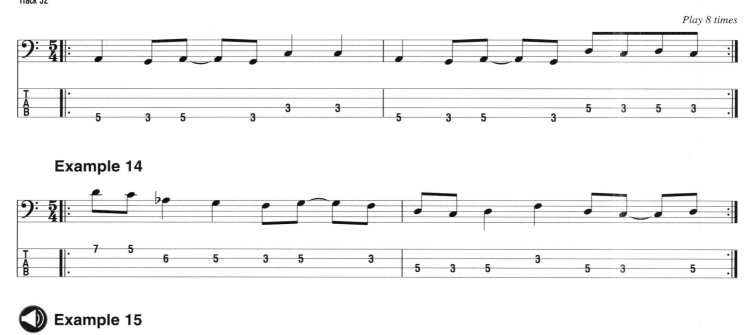

Example 14

Example 15

Track 33

7/4 Grooves and Sample Basslines

We can use the same 2/3 idea and use it with all other odd meter ideas. Now that we are dealing with 7/4, our grouping will be 2/2/3 or 3/2/2 (2+2+3=7!). Sometimes, this makes the pattern almost sound like a measure of 3 and a measure of 4, or vice versa. You could certainly also do a 2/3/2 pattern, but that's pretty rare.

The most famous 7/4 bassline in progressive rock (or all of rock, for that matter) is Pink Floyd's "Money." This bassline uses, that's right, a minor pentatonic scale (B minor pentatonic, to be exact). The rhythmic pattern is a 3/2/2 pattern. You can see something similar in Example 18.

Example 16: (2/2/3 PATTERN)

Example 17: (3/2/2 PATTERN)

Sample 7/4 Basslines

Example 18

Track 34

Play 8 times

Example 19

Play 8 times

Example 20

Track 35

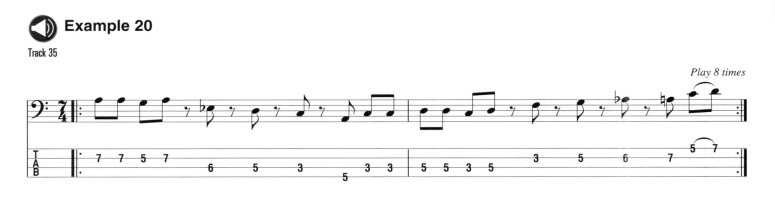

Play 8 times

9/4 and Beyond

Although there are certainly songs in 9/4, 11/4, 13/4, etc., they are usually thought of, or felt, more like groupings of measures than one long measure. For example, a measure of 9/4 is most likely going to be a two-measure phrase, with one measure of 4/4 and another of 5/4, or vice versa. It's really uncommon to see quarter-note-based time signatures larger than 7/4.

Suggested Listening

Here are some songs from various bands that demonstrate grooves and basslines in quarter-note-based odd meter (i.e., 5/4, 7/4, etc.). Some of these bands have been categorized in different genres than prog rock, but there's no doubting their influential use of odd meter.

Jethro Tull—"Living in the Past" (5/4)
Primus—"Here Come the Bastards" (5/4)
Soundgarden—"Outshined" (7/4)
Radiohead—"Paranoid Android" (includes 7/4)
Peter Gabriel—"Solsbury Hill" (7/4)
The Beatles—"All You Need is Love" (7/4)
Pink Floyd—"Money" (7/4)
Rush—"Xanadu" (includes 7/4)
Genesis—"Riding the Scree" (An actual 9/4 groove!)

Assignment

1. Play through each odd meter example. These simple-but-essential rhythmic grooves will help make these odd-meter phrases feel more natural.
2. Play through each of the sample basslines. Your initial practicing of assignment one will make these basslines easier to play.

8 Alternative Technique: Slap Playing

In this chapter we will be looking at one of the most exciting (and possibly *abused*!) bass techniques utilized in progressive rock: *slap bass*. Many people think of this as a funk technique, but please don't confuse the term "funk" with "slap." Sure, slap lines came about because of the percussive and syncopated sounds they produced in seventies funk and disco music, but using the slap technique doesn't necessarily make something funky. Likewise, you can sound super funky playing fingerstyle or with a pick. Although mostly associated with funk playing, you can use the slap bass technique in any style.

This technique, with its percussive sound, syncopated (against the beat) rhythms, and wide dynamic range (levels of volume and attack) is particularly useful in the progressive rock genre. In a musical style where anything goes and styles are mixed together in generous portions, the slap technique allows the progressive rock player a variety of sounds and ideas.

The reason I say that the slap technique is "abused" is that most bassists don't know how to truly play it. Most bassists will learn a few slap licks and play them *really* fast with no sense of time. Since they haven't put in the hours of practicing the technique in time, there are an awful lot of slap players out there really abusing the sound. Many slap players know a few cool slap lines, but then get frustrated that they don't or can't use the technique in a band situation. Even in the Musicians Institutes' Bass program, which teaches some of the finest players in the world, I find bassists have this challenge. They all practice their slap licks in class, but I rarely see them utilize the technique with a band.

I can also say that the technique was greatly abused in the 1980s, when slap bass was in its heyday. The mystery of the funky seventies' technique seemed to be solved, and it appeared that *everybody* was slapping and popping their way into a frenzy. Soon, producers, songwriters, music fans, and even bass players were feeling the technique was being a bit overused.

Today, it seems that, in the professional world, slap bass has found its place in a bass player's arsenal of sounds. It's a great tool to use to change up the dynamic, sound, attack, timbre, and yes, funkiness of a bassline. However, it may be a technique you use sparingly in order to keep the sound fresh. Even landmark slap-bass pioneers who have crossed over to mainstream pop success, like Level 42's Mark King and Red Hot Chili Peppers' Flea, have balanced their slap/pop pyrotechnics with truly inspired fingerstyle basslines. Although the music that these two bands and bass players play wouldn't be considered progressive rock, I would absolutely say that the way they play the bass is certainly progressive. To check out the technique used in progressive rock specifically, you can listen to players like Stanley Clarke, Les Claypool, Patrick O'Hearn, and Tony Levin, to name but a few.

To Slap or Not to Slap

Slap bass is a very exciting technique for bass players. Normally regulated to hang back and groove in the shadows, slapping on the bass takes the instrument from the background and brings it right in the listener's face. Finally, bassists can share the spotlight, normally reserved for guitarists, by jumping center stage and laying down that great, big slap solo that brings the house down. Of course, as I mentioned earlier, this technique is often overused and abused. Like all techniques, you should utilize slap bass playing only when it's the perfect fit for the song. Sometimes, it takes a long time to understand when to play a certain technique and when not to. Some bassists, once they learn a few slap grooves, try to fit slap bass in wherever they can, often to the detriment of the song. Used sparingly, your slapping technique will become a powerful weapon in your bass-playing arsenal.

Getting Started

Slap bass is a technique where you literally "slap" your thumb down on the strings to produce a percussive sound. You can also use any one of your fingers (the index finger being the most common) to pull up on the string and release it back to the neck. This sound is actually referred to as "popping." However, the whole sound of "slapping" and "popping" is covered under the term "slap bass."

This act of slapping and popping is a pretty unnatural thing to do with your plucking hand. Thus, in order to really use this sound in your bag o' tricks, you need to spend a lot of time and repetition in practicing the technique. Let's get to it then!

With your plucking hand, make a "thumb's up" sign. See below.

Now, bring your knuckles back by straightening out your fist, as shown below.

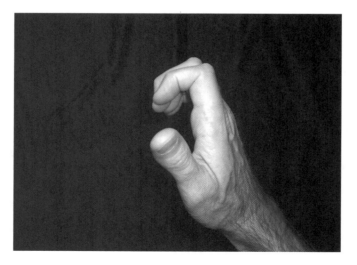

You'll notice that your fingers come away from your hand just slightly. That's perfect, as you will need a little space between your fingers and hand in order to grab the strings for popping.

All the Angles

There are two ways of angling your plucking hand in order to slap the strings. The way you choose will depend on how high or low your bass is strapped to your body. If your bass is near or above your belt, you will want your thumb to be perpendicular to the bass strings. Check it out here.

If your bass is near or below your waist, then it would be pretty uncomfortable to angle your hand in the way shown above. In this case, you would want your thumb to be parallel to the bass strings. See how this is done in the photo below.

This is why a player like Mark King, who wears his bass well above his waist, plays with his thumb perpendicular to the strings, and Flea, who wears his bass well below, plays with his thumb parallel to the strings. Both of these amazing slap bassists would have a *very* difficult time playing each other's bass due to this difference in hand placement.

So, if you don't particularly care if your bass is held high or low on your body, I would suggest that you wear your bass close to where it is when you are sitting down to practice. You don't want your bass to be in an altogether different spot from when you practice to when you are gigging. In this case, your thumb will be perpendicular to the strings. However, if you want to wear that bass down low, which any self-respecting, progressive-metal madman would almost *always* do, then you will want your thumb to be parallel.

For most of the pictures in this chapter, I will be showing you the perpendicular thumb. However, you can use either angle with the directions I give.

Okay, enough talk already! Let's get to some cool exercises and start enjoying this fun way to play the bass!

Exercises: Thumb Accuracy

Exercise 1: With your fret hand just barely touching your strings (to keep them from ringing), strike the E string with your thumb. You will want to use the middle area of your thumb. See the top photo to know where on your thumb to strike the string (notice my silly finger is pointing at the "sweet spot") and the middle photo to see how to actually strike the string.

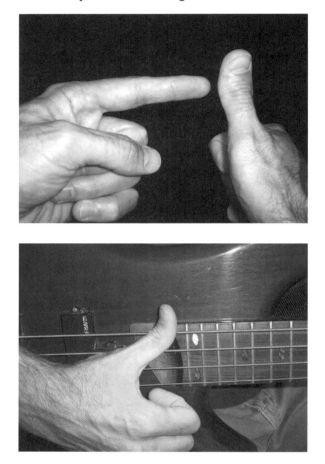

Make sure that you don't leave your thumb down on the string. Hit the string where the neck meets the body, and immediately lift your thumb off. You do *not* want to leave your thumb down on the string after you hit it. The first photo shows what to do, and the one on the next page shows you what *not* to do.

Thumb slightly off the string after striking

Thumb pushed and held down on the string after striking—*don't do this*!

Cool. Now hit the muted E string 8 times with your thumb. It should have a sharp, clicking sound to it. Remember, even though you are hitting it 8 times, you are counting "1–and–2–and–3–and–4–and." Then, move on to the A string and hit it with your thumb, counting "1–and–2–and–3–and–4–and" while you do it. Then, move on to the D and G strings.

At first, it will be a bit challenging to only hit the string you actually want to play without hitting another string as well. This is a bit frustrating, but just stay with it. You will improve your accuracy very quickly with focused practice.

When you finish with the G string, do the exercise again. This time, start with the G string and descend to the D, then A, and finally to the E string. Thus, your exercise will look like this:

Example 1: Muted-Thumb Exercise

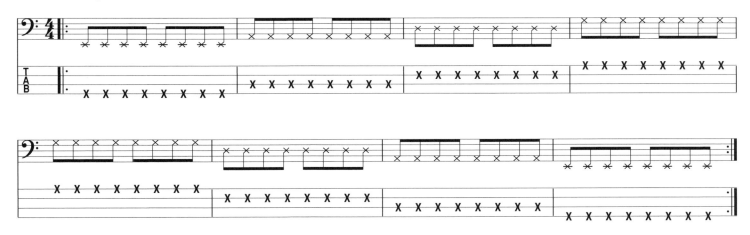

Get used to this method of practicing your slap technique. We'll always do the E string up to the G string, then repeat the G string, making our way back down to the E string. I know it may seem odd at first to do the G string twice in a row, but it'll make sense as you go on with the exercises.

Okay, so now let's do the same exercise, but instead of muting the notes, let the notes ring out.

Exercise 2: In the same way as you executed Exercise 1, hit each string 8 times. Only this time, don't mute the string you're hitting with your thumb. Let the string ring out in all its glory. You can mute the other strings with your fret hand if you'd like. With this exercise, you will *really* hear if you are not being accurate with your thumb, as the other notes you don't want to hit will ring out loud and clear, much to your dismay. Just be patient and work on your accuracy. Again, work on the E, A, D, and G strings, then go back down.

Not only should you look to only hit the string you want, you must also make sure that each string has the same volume. Normally, a beginning player will be able to hit the E and A strings pretty easily, but have a more difficult time with the D and G strings. This is because the strings are smaller, so they are harder to physically hit and don't produce the same amount of volume. You may find that you need to hit the D and G strings a little harder at first. This will help make the volume of all strings more consistent.

Example 2: Open-String Thumb Exercise

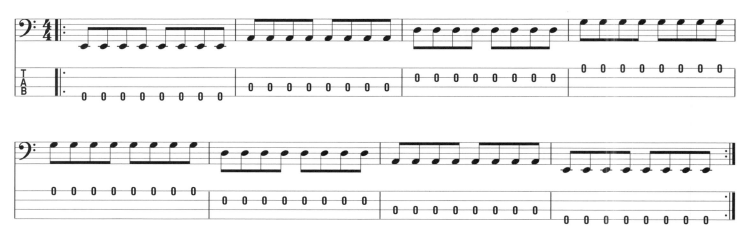

Work on these two exercises until you are able to hit each string accurately and produce a clean sound. Then, let's add some popping!

Slap Exercises: Popping

Place your first finger on the 5th fret, E string (A) and your fourth finger on 7th fret, D string (A) as shown.

With your thumb, strike the E string so you can hear the A note you are pressing down. Check it out here.

48

Notice in the previous picture that, after I hit the E string with my thumb, I'm still keeping my plucking hand down close to the strings. This is so I can reach under the D string with my index finger, pull the string up, and release it back down to the neck. Don't be shy—give it a good whack back onto the neck. This will produce a pretty loud, percussive "pop" sound on the higher A note. See below to see how it's done.

Well done! You have done your first true slap/pop movements. You rock! Let's turn it into a fun exercise, which you could actually use as a bass line.

Exercise 3: Play the A notes on the E and the D strings. Hit the low A (E string) with your thumb, then pull up on the high A (D string) and release the string so it slaps back down to the neck. After you have played the octave, go across the string to do the same thing with the D notes. Your low D will be on the A string (5th fret), and your high D will be on the G string (7th fret).

Example 3: Slap/Pop Octave Exercise

Do this exercise over and over until you can make it sound even. When it sounds even, play along with a metronome, drum machine, or some other time-keeping device. You *must* make sure that you can do all your slap exercises in time, or they will be useless parlor tricks you use at your local guitar store instead of a cool tool in your bass utility belt!

Slap Exercises: Hammer-Ons

Now that we've gotten our plucking hand more accurate at slapping and popping, let's add our fret hand. These next exercises are still going to work our plucking hand as well.

Put your first finger on A (5th fret) on the E string. See photo.

With your finger pressed down on the neck, slap the A note with your thumb. Then, hammer on with your pinky to the B note (7th fret). See photo.

You should be able to hear both notes (the one you slapped and the one you hammered on) with equal volume. This is kind of a cool technique since you are only slapping the string with your plucking hand once, and yet hearing two notes being played.

Exercise 4: Let's take this hammer-on thing across all the strings. You'll always be slapping the note on the 5th fret and hammering on to the note at the 7th fret.

Example 4: Hammer-On Exercise

Track 36

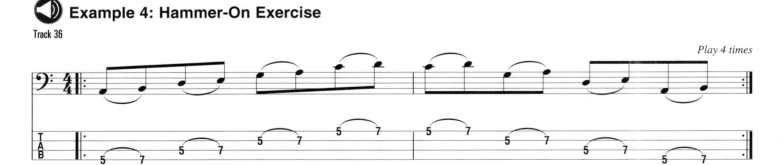

Folks, this exercise begins a series of exercises we'll be doing for slap. I can't tell you enough how crucial and beneficial this slap drill is. It will improve your thumb accuracy, timing, tone, and many other important aspects of slap playing. Make sure, when you do these exercises, that each note has the same volume and that you are playing the notes evenly in time. If you use a metronome, each note will be an eighth note (two notes per beat).

50

Exercise 5: This can be considered "Hammer-On Drill 2." Play the above exercise, but add a dead note after you play the hammer-on note. A dead note is where you slap the string, but hold your fretting hand lightly on the string to produce a muted sound (exactly as you played it in Exercise 1). The dead note is indicated with an "X."

Example 5: Hammer-On with Thumb Dead-Note Exercise

Track 37

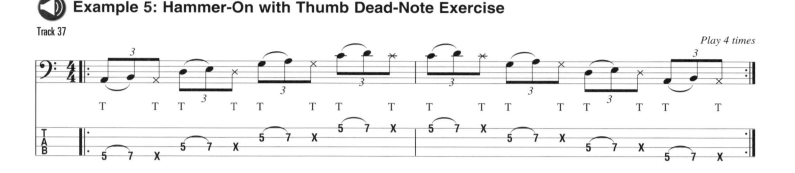

If you are playing this exercise with a metronome, you will now be playing three notes per beat (triplet). You can count it as "1–trip–let" or "tri–po–let."

Exercise 6: Play the above exercise, but actually pop your dead note instead of slapping it. You can pop any string you'd like, but it might be easier at first to pop the G string. Make sure you mute the G string when you pop it. It'll be a little tricky when you slap, hammer, *and* pop the G string, but with practice, it's got a very cool sound.

Example 6: Hammer-On with Popped Dead-Note Exercise

Track 38

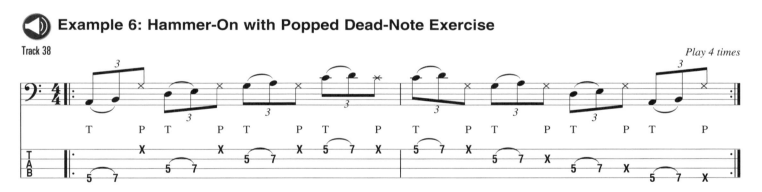

Exercise 7: This exercise is very similar to Exercise 5. After you play the hammer-on, you play two dead notes.

Example 7: Hammer-On with Two Thumb Dead-Note Exercise

Track 39

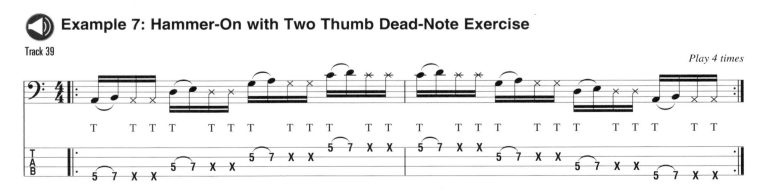

If you are playing this exercise with a metronome, you will now being playing four notes per beat, which is a sixteenth-note rhythm. You can count it as "1–ee–and–uh."

Exercise 8: This exercise is the same rhythm as Exercise 7. After you play the hammer-on, you are going to play two dead notes. This time, however, you are going to play the first dead note as a slap and the second one as a pop.

Example 8: Hammer-On with Octave Dead-Note Exercise

Track 40

Play 4 times

If you are playing this exercise with a metronome, you will again being playing four notes per beat, which is a sixteenth-note rhythm.

Slap Exercises: Pull-Offs

A *pull-off* is another very cool slap technique you can use. Think of it as the opposite of a hammer-on. Instead of slapping the A on the E string and hammering on to the B note, you will slap the B and pull your pinky off the string so you can hear the A note. Your first finger will always stay on the lower note. Check out the photos below.

Extra Exercises: You can do Exercises 4–8 but replace the hammer-on with the pull-off.

Sample Basslines

What's really cool about all the slap exercises in this chapter is that you can immediately use those ideas to create basslines. Check out the sample basslines below.

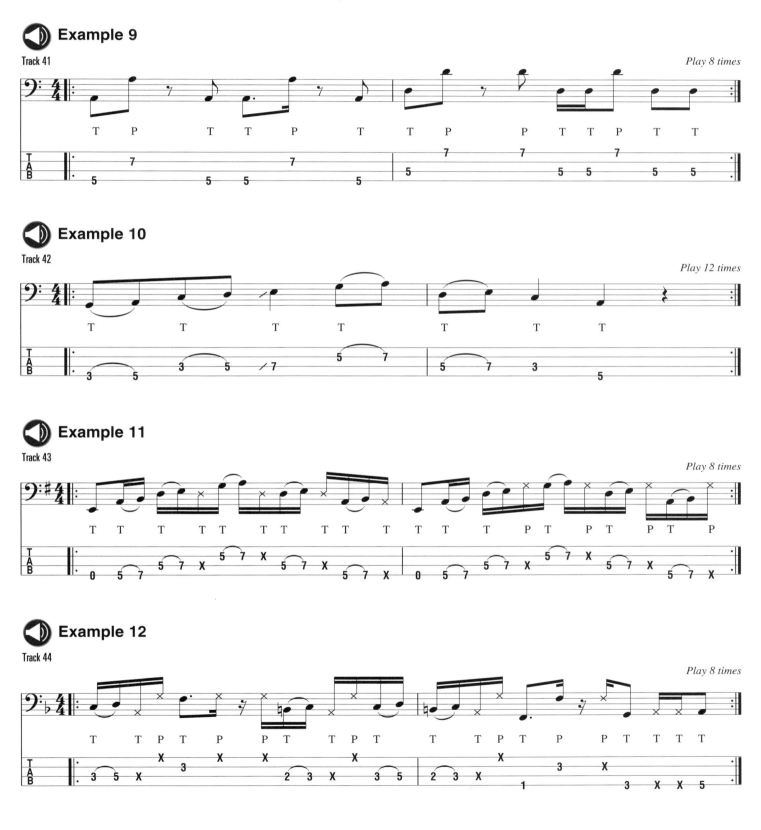

Example 9

Track 41

Play 8 times

Example 10

Track 42

Play 12 times

Example 11

Track 43

Play 8 times

Example 12

Track 44

Play 8 times

Example 13

Play 8 times

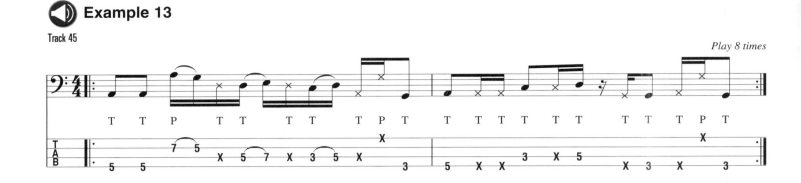

Please note that all of these basslines use the major pentatonic scale, the minor pentatonic/blues scale, or a combination of both. I told you those were some useful scales! Take some time now and create some of your own basslines.

There you go. This was quite an extensive chapter for us. There are lots of exercises in here, so make sure you take your time and really get these things sounding good. Please make sure that you listen to the CD as well, so you can hear how to play these exercises properly. Finally, once you get the basics of this technique, make sure you always, always, and *always* practice your slap playing with a *metronome*. The ability to play this in time is the number one reason why most bassists can't truly use slap playing in their everyday playing or band situations. Everything you need to build cool slap basslines is here in this chapter. Practice it in time, and you will be able to use these ideas immediately!

Assignment

1. Practice the octave exercises and the thumb accuracy exercises first (Exercises 1–3). Get these drills together so you can play them evenly and accurately. Speed is not important; just make sure they sound good. Once that is accomplished, you can work on increasing the speed.
2. Work on the Hammer-on Exercises (Exercises 4–8). These exercises are extremely important, as they involve a lot more focus on your fret-hand technique.
3. Try to change the Hammer-On exercises to Pull-Off exercises.
4. Learn some of the sample basslines. If you are a more advanced player, try playing them in different keys.
5. Using the ideas from the exercises and sample basslines, try creating your own slap lines.

Odd Meter: Crazy "8s"

If you have not yet gone through and learned the material from Chapter Seven (Odd Meter: Playing "4" Keeps), please do so now before you move on to this chapter. That material is essential for truly understanding the concepts laid out here. If you can understand and play the examples and sample basslines from there, this chapter will be a breeze!

The new concept we are adding is changing the grooves from a quarter-note pulse to an eighth-note pulse. Generally speaking, grooves with eighth-note pulses tend to sound faster than the ones based on quarter notes. Let's look at an odd-meter time signature as written with an eighth-note pulse.

5 —number of beats in a measure
8 —the note that gets the beat (in this case, 1/8 or the eighth note)

For the example above, there are 5 beats in the measure. Since the bottom number is an 8, the eighth note gets the beat. Thus, each measure will have 5 eighth notes (or the equivalent) in it.

Changing the Bottom Number

By changing the bottom number of the time signature, the value and the speed of the pulse changes. A 7/4 feel, since it has a quarter-note pulse, will sound slower than a 7/8 feel, which has an eighth-note pulse.

6/8 Grooves and Sample Basslines

Let's take a look at 6/8 patterns. We are starting with this because it is the most common of the eighth-note meters. This groove has a strong two-pulse with a feel of ONE–two–three–FOUR–five–six.

Example 1

Example 2

55

Sample 6/8 Basslines

Example 3

Track 46

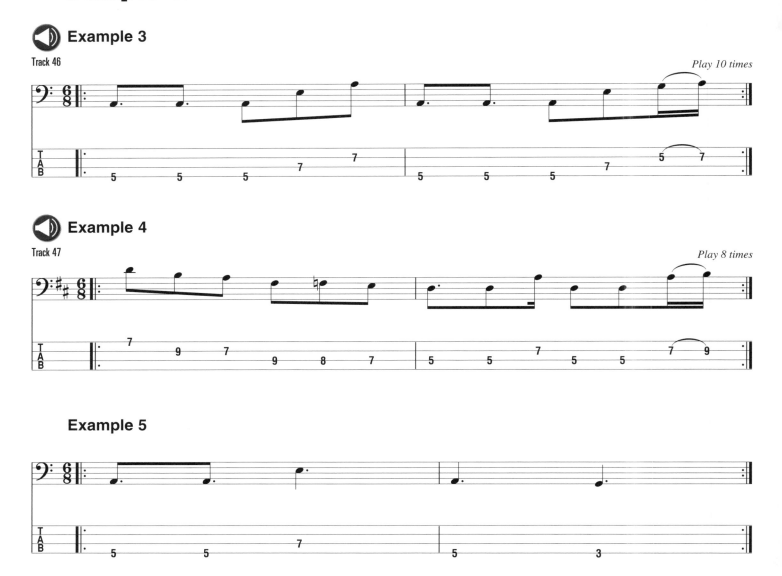

Example 4

Track 47

Example 5

5/8 Grooves and Sample Basslines

Remember the 2/3 concept from Chapter Seven? Again, we can break down the grouping of 5 into a groups of 2 and 3 (2 + 3 = 5!). You can either think of groupings of 5 as a 2/3 or 3/2 pattern. Let's look at a 2/3 pattern.

Example 6

Here's another very important concept from Chapter Seven. Remember that if we play a dotted-quarter-note rhythm in the 3/4 measure, we will have two rhythms of equal value. Well, we can do this same thing in 5/8 and 7/8 basslines. Instead of dotted-quarter notes, we'll now use dotted-eighth notes. The concept and the feel is essentially the same as before.

Example 7

Track 48

Play 8 times

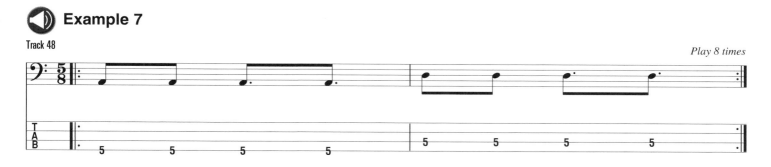

Let's switch the pattern and play a few things with a 3/2 feel.

Example 8

Example 9

Track 49

Play 10 times

Sample 5/8 Basslines

Once again, we are using a combination of major and minor pentatonic scales to create these basslines.

Example 10

Track 50

Play 8 times

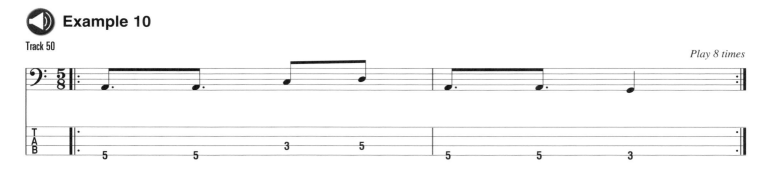

Example 11

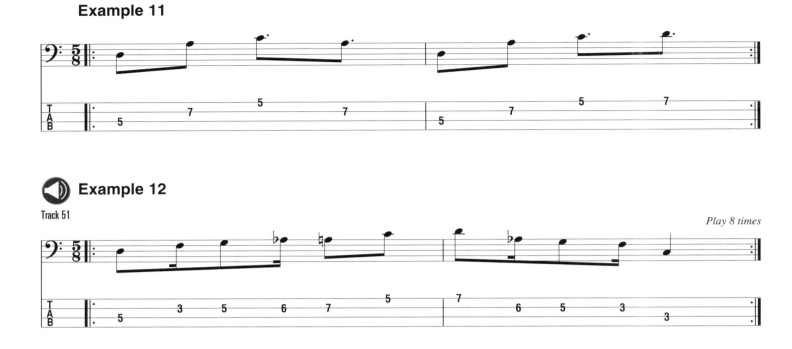

Example 12

Track 51

Play 8 times

7/8 Grooves and Sample Basslines

We can use the same 2/3 idea and use it with all other odd-meter ideas. However, now that we are dealing with 7/8, our grouping will be 2/2/3 or 3/2/2 (2+2+3=7). The dotted notes break up the groove nicely and keep it from sound too "odd meterish."

Example 13

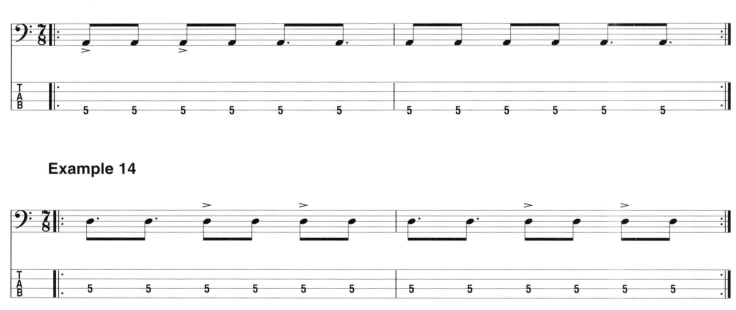

Example 14

Sample 7/8 Basslines

🔊 **Example 15**

Track 52

Play 8 times

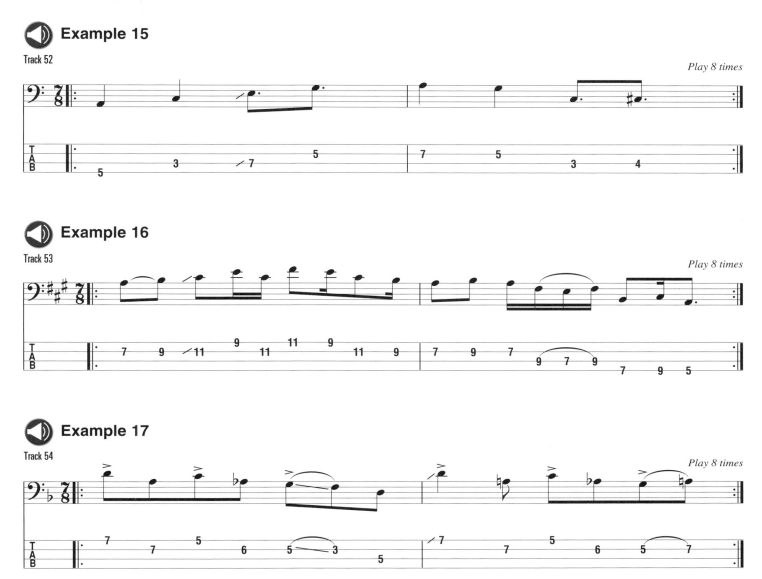

🔊 **Example 16**

Track 53

Play 8 times

🔊 **Example 17**

Track 54

Play 8 times

9/8 Grooves and Sample Basslines

You know the drill. Let's get to it! We'll look at the two most popular patterns, the 2/2/2/3 and 3/3/3 patterns. This time for the twos, we'll play quarter notes instead of eighth notes. This helps the groove flow a little more.

Example 18

Example 19

Sample 9/8 Basslines

Example 20

Track 55

Example 21

Track 56

Example 22

Track 57

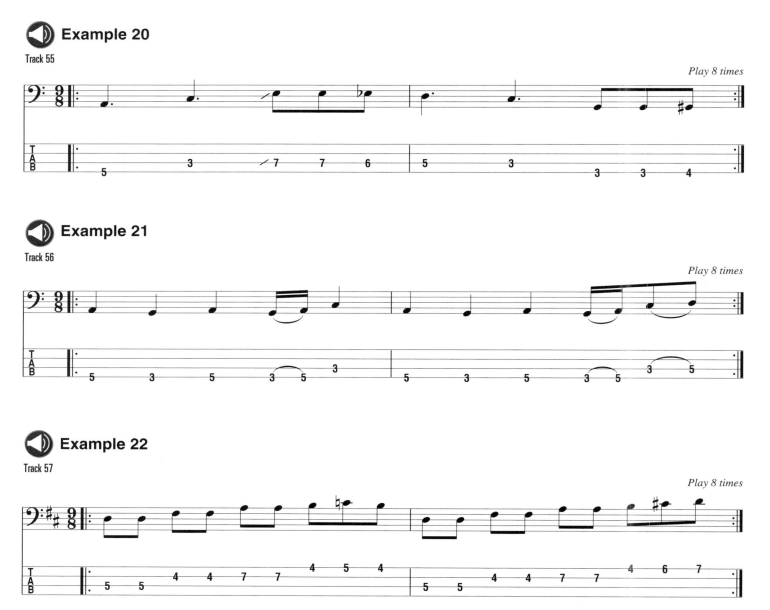

Suggested Listening

These songs all have some odd-meter sections in them. Check them out for further inspiration:

Jethro Tull—"Thick as a Brick" (6/8)
Lalo Schifrin—Theme from "Mission Impossible" (5/8)
King Crimson—"Frame by Frame" (7/8)
Sting—"Seven Days" (5/8)
Rush—"Tom Sawyer" (Solo in 7/8)
Porcupine Tree—"Fear of a Blank Planet" (Bridge in 5/8)
Genesis—"Supper's Ready (Apocalypse in 9/8)"
Genesis—"Dance on a Volcano" (7/8)
Yes—"Hold On" (12/8)

Assignment

1. Play through each odd-meter example. These simple-but-essential rhythmic grooves will help make these odd-meter phrases feel more natural.
2. Play through each of the sample basslines. Your initial practice of assignment one will make these basslines easier to play.

Alternative Technique: Chord Playing

One of the major differences between playing guitar and bass is that you don't play chords on the bass. The range of notes on the bass would make a chord sound muddy and unclear. Normally, the bass *implies* chords by playing each individual note of the chord, known as an *arpeggio*. However, we can utilize some chord shapes from the guitar onto the bass. This will allow us to maintain a low bass note, but also add harmony to our sound. This is very useful in bands that only have one harmony instrument (i.e., keyboards or a power trio).

One cool thing about all these chords that you will learn is that they are movable shapes. For example, if you take a major seven chord shape with the lowest note C, you will have a Cma7 chord. If you play the same exact shape with the lowest note F$\sharp$, you will have an F$\sharp$ma7 chord. These movable shapes make it easy to learn and use these chords quickly.

Power Chords

A great way to start playing chordally is to use the power chords. This is where you play the root and the 5th together. While this usually sounds best on thinner strings (D and G strings), this sound works with a root on the E or A string as well. Power chords are very useful because you can use these chords over both major and minor chords, since they only use the root and 5th. On the staff, the chord is written with a "5" after the letter name.

G5 chord with the root on the D string (5th fret).

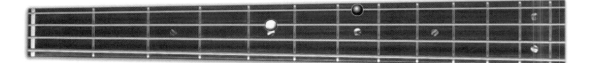

G5 chord with the root on the A string (10th fret). Notice how much "darker" this sounds than the previous chord.

G5 chord with the root on the E string (3rd fret). Not only is this chord played on a thicker string, but the notes are also an octave below the other two examples.

You can add the root's octave to make a three-note power chord. You can only use this on the E and A string roots.

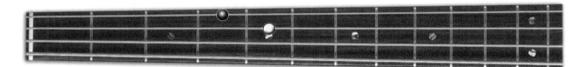

Thirds

If you want to add a little more substance to your chordal playing, you should include the 3rd of the chord. The 3rd is the note that gives the chord its major or minor sound. Again, these chords sound best played with the root on the D string, but it also works with the root on the A string if you play it high enough on the neck.

G Major Chord with the Root on the D String (5th Fret)

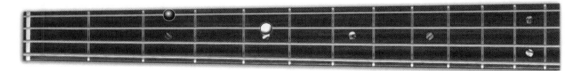

G Minor Chord with the Root on the D String (5th Fret)

G Major Chord with the Root on the A String (10th Fret)

G Minor Chord with the Root on the A String (10th Fret)

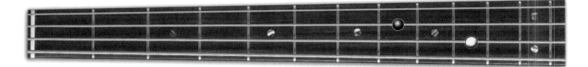

If you played this shape with the root on the E string, it would sound very muddy. However, if we take the 3rd and play it up the octave, it sounds much more clear. You will also be able to play a lower-sounding root, and there is a lot of separation between the lower and higher notes.

G Major Chord with the Root on the E String (3rd Fret)

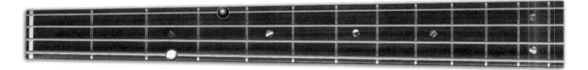

G Minor Chord with the Root on the E String (3rd Fret)

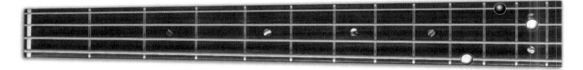

Another interesting thing to try is to add the octave to this shape. This adds more depth to the chord. This might be tough to play if you have smaller fingers, so let's try it up the neck first.

D Major Chord with the Root on the E String (10th Fret) and the Octave Added

D Minor Chord with the Root on the E String (10th Fret) and the Octave Added

Three-Note Seven Chords

To make our chords have a more specific sound, we can add the interval of a 7th to our root and 3rd. Here's some information to get your started:

1. *Major Seven Chord*: a major triad with a major 7th
2. *Dominant Seven Chord*: a major triad with a minor 7th
3. *Minor Seven Chord*: a minor triad with a minor 7th

These chords are pretty similar, as you only need to change one note to get a totally different sound. There are many more types of chords, but these three are the ones you will encounter the most. You can voice the chords with the roots on either the E or A string.

Roots on the E String

For these diagrams, the note on the lower string will be the root. These are also movable shapes. You may want to play all these shapes above the 12th fret to avoid having it sound too muddy.

Major Seven   Dominant Seven   Minor Seven

Roots on the A String

Major Seven   Dominant Seven   Minor Seven

Chord Chart

Here are all the chords we've discussed in this chapter, as well as some other useful chord types and shapes. You can play these shapes on any root and anywhere on the neck, but they sound best above the 12th fret.

E-String Roots

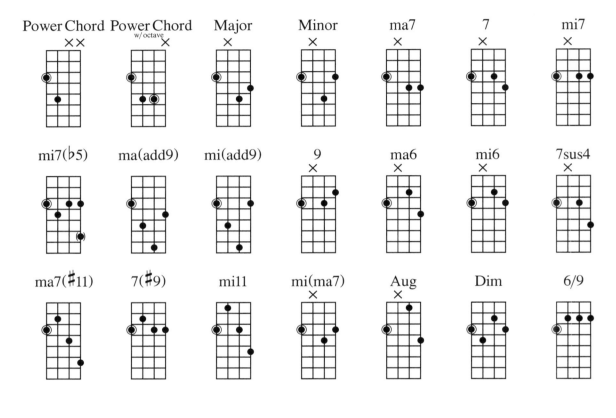

A-String Roots

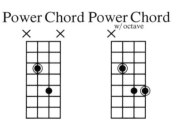
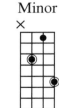

Sample Chord Progressions

The best way to *really* get these shapes under your fingers is to play them as part of a chord progression. Below you will see some sample progressions that will help you memorize the main chord shapes (power chords, triads, and seven chords). With each progression, try them with different voicings. For example, when you see a G major chord, try to play it with the roots on as many strings as possible.

There are some shortcuts to writing certain chord progressions. They are listed below:

Power Chord (Ex., C5).
Major Triad (Ex., C).
Minor Triad (Ex., Cmi, Cmin, C-—we'll use Cmi).
Major Seven (Ex., Cmaj7, Cma7, CΔ7—we'll use Cma7).
Dominant Seven (Ex., C7).
Minor Seven (Ex., Cmin7, Cmi7, C-7—we'll use Cmi7).

Note: You can play these chords with a pick (easy with power chords) or by plucking upwards with your thumb, index, and middle fingers.

Example 1: Power Chords Only

Example 2: Major and Minor Triads

Example 3: Seven Chords

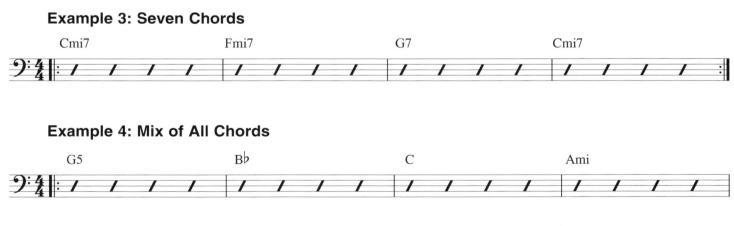

Example 4: Mix of All Chords

Sample Basslines

Who's to say that you can't play a bassline and a chord as well. Below you will see a few basslines that incorporate playing two or more notes.

Example 5

Track 58

Play 8 times

Example 6

Track 59

Play 8 times

Example 7: For this example, play the two chord tones with your index and middle fingers, and keep the low note moving with your thumb. It's a little tricky, but this is a great way to play chords and basslines at the same time.

Track 60

Play 8 times

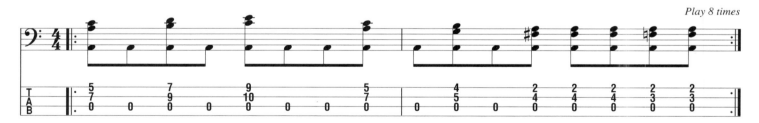

Assignment

1. Take your time to learn the shapes of the individual chords. Make sure each note in the chord sounds good (i.e., your finger is pushing the string down properly, etc.). Play the chords on different roots and different strings.
2. Play through the sample chord progressions. As mentioned before, this is the quickest way to really learn and play these shapes.
3. Play through and enjoy the sample basslines.

Other Useful Scales

Before rock 'n' roll, the harmony used in popular music was pretty sophisticated. In fact, many of the songs that are considered jazz standards today were actually pop songs in their day. Rock 'n' roll is derived from the blues, which uses simpler harmonies. As rock got more progressive in the late sixties and early seventies, so did the kind of harmony the musicians were writing with. Instead of simple diatonic harmony, many prog rock bands started using modal harmony. The chords became more sophisticated, and so did the scales used to create melodies and (in our specific case) basslines. Although the major and minor pentatonic scales you learned earlier in this book are very useful, you won't be able to play more sophisticated progressive rock music without knowledge of the aforementioned scales and modes. This final chapter will take a brief look at those scales and offer some fun and challenging sample basslines to play.

Note: You are only given the patterns in one octave. Try to extend these patterns above and below the octave once you are comfortable with the scale.

Lydian Mode

Please refer to Chapter Four for the different major scale patterns. If we take the 4th note of the major scale and raise it by a half step, we create the *Lydian* mode. This gives our "happy" sounding major scale a little more of an "outside" sound.

A Lydian Mode Starting on the E String with the 2nd Finger

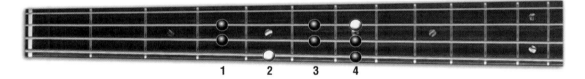

A Lydian Mode Starting on the E String with the 4th Finger

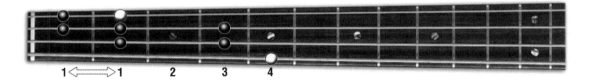

🔊 **Example 1: Sample Lydian Bassline**

Track 61

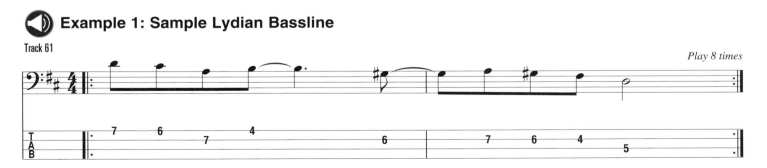

Minor Scale and Dorian Mode

The minor scale has many descriptive words that go with it (i.e., sad, dark). This feeling comes from the minor 3rd and minor 7th degree of the scale, but the note that usually pulls at the heartstrings is the minor 6th degree. This scale, also referred to as "natural minor," is a very common scale to use in all styles. Please refer to Chapter Five for the different patterns of the minor scale.

The Dorian mode is one of the most widely-used scales of all styles. It has the minor quality with the minor 3rd and 7th. It differs from the minor scale because it has a major 6th interval. That means the 6th scale degree is a half step higher in the Dorian mode. This raised 6th gives Dorian a minor sound without it being so sad or dark.

A Dorian Mode Starting on the E String with the 1st Finger

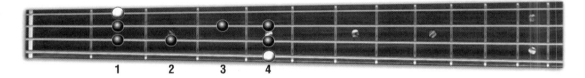

A Dorian Scale Starting on the E String with the 4th Finger

Example 2: Sample Dorian Bassline (with blues note thrown in for fun!)

Track 62

Dominant Scales

The following scales will all work over dominant chords—that is, major triads with minor 7ths. There are many scales that you can play over dominant chords, but we will focus on the most widely-used ones.

Dominant chords are used to create tension in a chord progression. The mix of the major 3rd and the minor 7th intervals create a *tritone*, which is a very tense-sounding interval. In medieval times, this interval created the "Devil's Chord," and you could be put to death for playing it! Nice thing that people have loosened up a bit!

With every dominant scale we look at, they will progressively get more "out" sounding.

Mixolydian Mode

The Mixolydian mode is a great one to play over dominant chords. Basically, it's a major scale with a minor 7th note. This is the go-to scale for blues basslines.

Chords to use Mixolydian with: dominant sevens and dominant nines.

A Mixolydian Mode Starting on the E String with the 2nd Finger

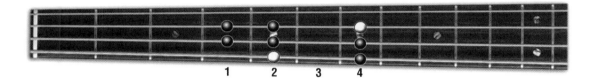

A Mixolydian Mode Starting on the E String with the 4th Finger

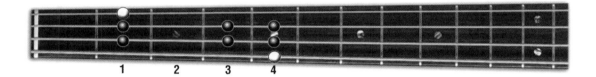

Example 3: Sample Mixolydian Bassline

Track 63

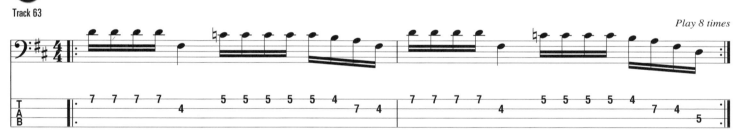

Lydian ♭7 Scale

Although the Lydian mode is used over major seven chords, the Lydian ♭7 scale is used for dominant seven chords. This scale could actually be called the "Mixolydian ♯4," but it's not. The raised 4th degree gives this dominant scale a more "open" and "out" sound than its Mixolydian brother.

Chords to use Lydian ♭7 scale with: dominant sevens, dominant nines, and dominant seven (♯11).

A Lydian ♭7 Scale Starting on the E String with the 2nd Finger

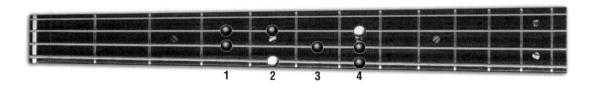

71

A Lydian ♭7 Scale Starting on the E String with the 4th Finger

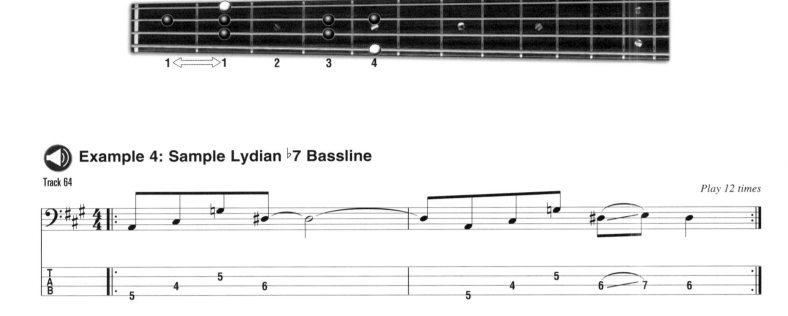

1 ⟷ 1   2   3   4

Example 4: Sample Lydian ♭7 Bassline

Track 64

Play 12 times

Whole-Tone Scale

This scale is similar to the Lydian ♭7 in that it has both the ♯4th and the ♭7th. In addition, there is also a ♯5 or ♭6 (♭13) in this scale. As the name implies, this is a scale built on whole steps. Because of that, this scale has only six notes instead of the usual seven.

Chords to use whole-tone with: dominant seven (♯5), dominant nine (♯5), dominant seven (♯11), and dominant seven (♭13).

A Whole-Tone Scale Starting on the E String with the 2nd Finger

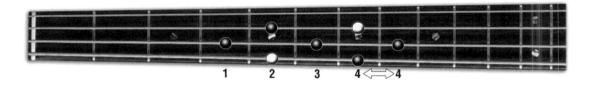

1   2   3   4 ⟷ 4

A Whole-Tone Scale Starting on the E String with the 4th Finger

1 ⟷ 1   2   3   4

Example 5: Sample Whole-Tone Bassline

Track 65

Play 12 times

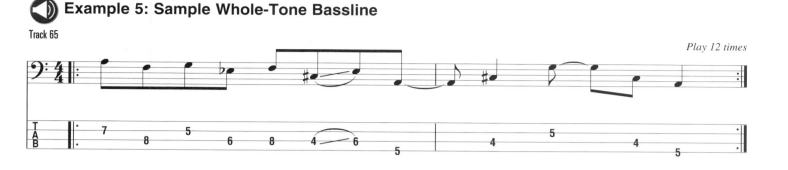

Altered Scale

This scale is actually a mode of the melodic minor scale. This scale continues in our progression of "out" sounding scales by having the $\sharp$4th, $\sharp$5th, and $\flat$7th, while adding a $\flat$2nd and $\sharp$2nd ($\flat$9th and $\sharp$9th).

Chords to use Altered scale with: dominant seven ($\sharp$5), dominant seven ($\flat$9 or $\sharp$9), dominant seven ($\sharp$11), dominant seven ($\flat$5 or $\sharp$5), dominant seven ($\flat$13), and dominant seven ($\sharp$9, $\sharp$5).

A Altered Scale Starting on the E String with the 1st Finger

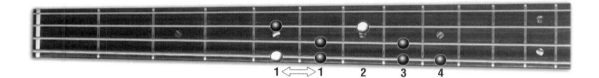

A Altered Scale Starting on the E String with the 3rd Finger

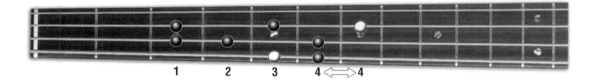

Example 6: Sample Altered Bassline

Track 66

Play 16 times

73

Dominant Diminished Scale

This scale is also widely known as the "half-whole" scale. If you can remember that name, you will know how to play this scale. It is a series of notes with a half-whole-step pattern. Because of this, the dominant diminished scale is one of the rare scales that actually has eight notes in it (not including the octave). This scale is very similar to the Altered scale, except this scale has a natural 5 and 6.

Chords to use dominant diminished scale with: dominant seven, dominant seven ($\flat$9 or $\sharp$9), dominant seven ($\sharp$11), and dominant thirteen.

A Dominant Diminished Scale Starting on the E String with the 1st Finger

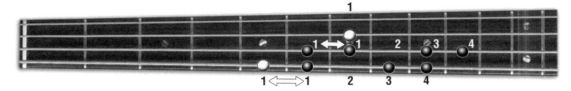

A Dominant Diminished Scale Starting on the E String with the 3rd Finger

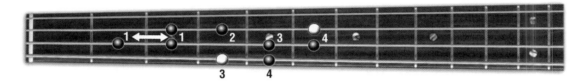

Example 7: Sample Dominant Diminished Scale Bassline

Track 67

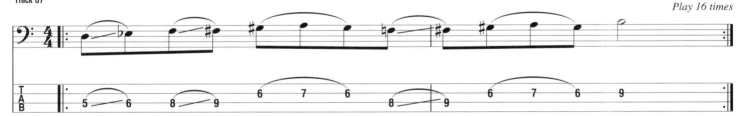

Assignment

1. Working in the order which they were presented in this chapter, memorize each scale. You can work everything starting on A on the E string, but then play the scale with different roots. Once you feel comfortable with a particular scale, start improvising with it and create your own basslines and riffs.

2. Learn and play along with each sample bassline. You can do this after you learn the scale shapes, but before you start improvising. These samples can help you get started with creating your own ideas.

74

Final Thoughts

I hope that you have found this book useful. I think this is much more than just a book on learning how to play progressive rock. I truly think that if you can play and understand all the concepts in this book, you will be well on your way to being a great bassist, regardless of style. As I said in the introduction, think of yourself as a progressive bass player. Never be afraid of pushing the boundaries of the instrument. At the same time, remember that the bass has an essential rhythmic, sonic, and harmonic function in a rock band. Juggling these responsibilities while playing the instrument in new or unorthodox ways will be an interesting challenge for you.

Remember to go through the examples and sample basslines very slowly. Get these lines under your fingers before you play along with the recordings. If the recordings are too fast to play along with at first, simply play the examples slowly at first. You will be able to get them up to speed pretty quickly.

Feel free to get in touch with me about your progress or questions you may have. You can e-mail me through my website at *www.christophermaloney.com*.

Acknowledgments

I'd like to give a big thanks to Jeff Schroedl, Kurt Plahna, and everyone at Hal Leonard Publishing for their support of not only this book, but all books written by instructors of the Musicians Institute. Thanks also to Keith Wyatt, Alexis Skljarevski, Dave Keif, and Dominic Hauser for helping me get started with this endeavor. Thanks to Dan Maske for his book *Progressive Rock Keyboards* and Dino Monoxelos for his book *Odd Meter Bassics*, both of which were great resources for me. Thanks to my Cosmosquad brethren Jeff Kollman and Shane Gaalaas for their fantastic playing and friendship throughout the years, and on the recorded examples in this book. Thanks to all the great teachers who have passed on their musical knowledge and experience to me, including Gordon Moore, Thomas Reitano, Steven Culhane, Stan Gosek, Dale Titus, and all the great players and instructors at Musicians Institute. Thanks also to all the great prog rock bands who have inspired my bass playing and songwriting. And finally, thanks to my loving and supportive family: my fiancé Kristina Balobeck, my daughter Amanda, my parents John and Janet Maloney, and the Maloneys of Victor!

About the Author

Christopher Maloney is a professional bassist, as well as singer/songwriter. He has toured around the world and has recorded and performed with notable musicians such as Dweezil Zappa, Ahmet Zappa, Virgil Donati, Jeff Kollman, Hardline, Lisa Loeb, Chieli Minucci, Phil Mogg, Brett Garsed and members of Journey, Savage Garden, and INXS. In addition to recording scores of CDs as a sideman for other artists, Maloney has released two solo CDs on the Sunset Records label, *Control* and *The Terrors of Intimacy*.

He is a three-time ASCAP Awards winner, and his songs have been licensed on radio and television throughout the world. His instrumental band, Cosmosquad, has released several CDs and the live DVD *Lights...Camera... SQUAD!* Maloney is also an artist and clinician for Fender Musical Instruments, SWR Amplifiers, Carvin Instruments, and D'Addario Strings. He has Bachelor's Degrees in Music and Communications from Oswego State University and a Vocational Honors Certificate from the world-renowned Musicians Institute (MI), where he was named

the "Outstanding Student of the Year." In addition to his recording and touring duties, Maloney enjoys his time as an instructor at MI. He is also working on opening a private lesson studio in Jupiter, Florida called Absolute Music Studios.

Bass Notation Legend

Bass music can be notated two different ways: on a *musical staff*, and in *tablature*.

THE MUSICAL STAFF shows pitches and rhythms and is divided by bar lines into measures. Pitches are named after the first seven letters of the alphabet.

TABLATURE graphically represents the bass fingerboard. Each horizontal line represents a string, and each number represents a fret.

3rd string, open   2nd string, 2nd fret   1st & 2nd strings open, played together

HAMMER-ON: Strike the first (lower) note with one finger, then sound the higher note (on the same string) with another finger by fretting it without picking.

PULL-OFF: Place both fingers on the notes to be sounded. Strike the first note and without picking, pull the finger off to sound the second (lower) note.

LEGATO SLIDE: Strike the first note and then slide the same fret-hand finger up or down to the second note. The second note is not struck.

SHIFT SLIDE: Same as legato slide, except the second note is struck.

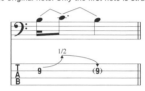

TRILL: Very rapidly alternate between the notes indicated by continuously hammering on and pulling off.

TREMOLO PICKING: The note is picked as rapidly and continuously as possible.

VIBRATO: The string is vibrated by rapidly bending and releasing the note with the fretting hand.

SHAKE: Using one finger, rapidly alternate between two notes on one string by sliding either a half-step above or below.

NATURAL HARMONIC: Strike the note while the fret hand lightly touches the string directly over the fret indicated.

MUFFLED STRINGS: A percussive sound is produced by laying the fret hand across the string(s) without depressing them and striking them with the pick hand.

BEND: Strike the note and bend up the interval shown.

BEND AND RELEASE: Strike the note and bend up as indicated, then release back to the original note. Only the first note is struck.

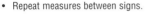

RIGHT-HAND TAP: Hammer ("tap") the fret indicated with the "pick-hand" index or middle finger and pull off to the note fretted by the fret hand.

LEFT-HAND TAP: Hammer ("tap") the fret indicated with the "fret-hand" index or middle finger.

SLAP: Strike ("slap") string with right-hand thumb.

POP: Snap ("pop") string with right-hand index or middle finger.

Additional Musical Definitions

(accent)	•	Accentuate note (play it louder).
(accent)	•	Accentuate note with great intensity.
(staccato)	•	Play the note short.
⊓	•	Downstroke
∨	•	Upstroke
D.S. al Coda	•	Go back to the sign (𝄋), then play until the measure marked "*To Coda*," then skip to the section labelled "**Coda**."

D.C. al Fine	•	Go back to the beginning of the song and play until the measure marked "*Fine*" (end).
Bass Fig.	•	Label used to recall a recurring pattern.
Fill	•	Label used to identify a brief melodic figure which is to be inserted into the arrangement.
tacet	•	Instrument is silent (drops out).
	•	Repeat measures between signs.
	•	When a repeated section has different endings, play the first ending only the first time and the second ending only the second time.

NOTE: Tablature numbers in parentheses mean:
1. The note is being sustained over a system (note in standard notation is tied), or
2. The note is sustained, but a new articulation (such as a hammer-on, pull-off, slide or vibrato) begins, or
3. The note is a barely audible "ghost" note (note in standard notation is also in parentheses).

77

MUSICIANS INSTITUTE PRESS is the official series of Southern California's renowned music school, Musicians Institute. MI instructors, some of the finest musicians in the world, share their vast knowledge and experience with you – no matter what your current level. For guitar, bass, drums, vocals, and keyboards, MI Press offers the finest music curriculum for higher learning through a variety of series:

ESSENTIAL CONCEPTS
Designed from MI core curriculum programs.

MASTER CLASS
Designed from MI elective courses.

PRIVATE LESSONS
Tackle a variety of topics "one-on one" with MI faculty instructors.

BASS

Arpeggios for Bass
by Dave Keif • **Private Lessons**
00695133 . . . . $14.95

The Art of Walking Bass
by Bob Magnusson • **Master Class**
00695168 Book/CD Pack $18.95

Bass Fretboard Basics
by Paul Farnen • **Essential Concepts**
00695201 . . . . $16.95

Bass Playing Techniques
by Alexis Sklarevski • **Essential Concepts**
00695207 . . . . $16.95

Chords for Bass
by Dominik Hauser • **Master Class**
00695934 Book/CD Pack $16.95

Groove Mastery
by Oneida James • **Private Lessons**
00695771 Book/CD Pack $17.95

Grooves for Electric Bass
by David Keif • **Private Lessons**
00695265 Book/CD Pack $15.99

Latin Bass
by George Lopez and David Keif • **Private Lessons**
00695543 Book/CD Pack $15.99

Music Reading for Bass
by Wendy Wrehovcsik • **Essential Concepts**
00695203 . . . . $10.95

GUITAR

Advanced Guitar Soloing
by Daniel Gilbert & Beth Marlis • **Essential Concepts**
00695636 Book/CD Pack $19.95

Advanced Scale Concepts & Licks for Guitar
by Jean Marc Belkadi • **Private Lessons**
00695298 Book/CD Pack $16.95

Basic Blues Guitar
by Steve Trovato • **Private Lessons**
00695180 Book/CD Pack $15.99

Blues/Rock Soloing for Guitar
by Robert Calva • **Private Lessons**
00695680 Book/CD Pack $18.95

Blues Rhythm Guitar
by Keith Wyatt • **Master Class**
00695131 Book/CD Pack $19.95

Dean Brown
00696002 DVD $29.95

Chord Progressions for Guitar
by Tom Kolb • **Private Lessons**
00695664 Book/CD Pack $16.95

Chord Tone Soloing
by Barrett Tagliarino • **Private Lessons**
00695855 Book/CD Pack $22.95

Chord-Melody Guitar
by Bruce Buckingham • **Private Lessons**
00695646 Book/CD Pack $16.95

Prices, contents, and availability subject to change without notice.
FOR MORE INFORMATION, SEE YOUR LOCAL MUSIC DEALER,
OR WRITE TO:

HAL•LEONARD®
C O R P O R A T I O N
7777 W. BLUEMOUND RD. P.O. BOX 13819 MILWAUKEE, WI 53213

www.halleonard.com

Classical & Fingerstyle Guitar Techniques
by David Oakes • **Master Class**
00695171 Book/CD Pack $16.95

Classical Themes for Electric Guitar
by Jean Marc Belkadi • **Private Lessons**
00695806 Book/CD Pack $15.99

Contemporary Acoustic Guitar
by Eric Paschal & Steve Trovato • **Master Class**
00695320 Book/CD Pack $16.95

Creative Chord Shapes
by Jamie Findlay • **Private Lessons**
00695172 Book/CD Pack $10.99

Diminished Scale for Guitar
by Jean Marc Belkadi • **Private Lessons**
00695227 Book/CD Pack $10.99

Essential Rhythm Guitar
by Steve Trovato • **Private Lessons**
00695181 Book/CD Pack $15.99

Ethnic Rhythms for Electric Guitar
by Jean Marc Belkadi • **Private Lessons**
00695873 Book/CD Pack $17.99

Exotic Scales & Licks for Electric Guitar
by Jean Marc Belkadi • **Private Lessons**
00695860 Book/CD Pack $16.95

Funk Guitar
by Ross Bolton • **Private Lessons**
00695419 Book/CD Pack $15.99

Guitar Basics
by Bruce Buckingham • **Private Lessons**
00695134 Book/CD Pack $17.95

Guitar Fretboard Workbook
by Barrett Tagliarino • **Essential Concepts**
00695712 . . . . $17.99

Guitar Hanon
by Peter Deneff • **Private Lessons**
00695321 . . . . $9.95

Guitar Lick•tionary
by Dave Hill • **Private Lessons**
00695482 Book/CD Pack $18.95

Guitar Soloing
by Dan Gilbert & Beth Marlis • **Essential Concepts**
00695190 Book/CD Pack $19.95
00695907 DVD $19.95

Harmonics
by Jamie Findlay • **Private Lessons**
00695169 Book/CD Pack $13.99

Introduction to Jazz Guitar Soloing
by Joe Elliott • **Master Class**
00695406 Book/CD Pack $19.95

Jazz Guitar Chord System
by Scott Henderson • **Private Lessons**
00695291 . . . . $10.95

Jazz Guitar Improvisation
by Sid Jacobs • **Master Class**
00695128 Book/CD Pack $18.99
00695908 DVD $19.95
00695639 VHS Video $19.95

Jazz-Rock Triad Improvising
by Jean Marc Belkadi • **Private Lessons**
00695361 Book/CD Pack $15.99

Latin Guitar
by Bruce Buckingham • **Master Class**
00695379 Book/CD Pack $16.95

Modern Approach to Jazz, Rock & Fusion Guitar
by Jean Marc Belkadi • **Private Lessons**
00695143 Book/CD Pack $15.99

Modern Jazz Concepts for Guitar
by Sid Jacobs • **Master Class**
00695711 Book/CD Pack $16.95

Modern Rock Rhythm Guitar
by Danny Gill • **Private Lessons**
00695682 Book/CD Pack $16.95

Modes for Guitar
by Tom Kolb • **Private Lessons**
00695555 Book/CD Pack $17.95

Music Reading for Guitar
by David Oakes • **Essential Concepts**
00695192 . . . . $19.99

The Musician's Guide to Recording Acoustic Guitar
by Dallan Beck • **Private Lessons**
00695505 Book/CD Pack $13.99

Outside Guitar Licks
by Jean Marc Belkadi • **Private Lessons**
00695697 Book/CD Pack $15.95

Power Plucking
by Dale Turner • **Private Lesson**
00695962 . . . . $19.95

Practice Trax for Guitar
by Danny Gill • **Private Lessons**
00695601 Book/CD Pack $17.99

Progressive Tapping Licks
by Jean Marc Belkadi • **Private Lessons**
00695748 Book/CD Pack $15.95

Rhythm Guitar
by Bruce Buckingham & Eric Paschal • **Essential Concepts**
00695188 Book $17.95
00695644 VHS Video $19.95

Rock Lead Basics
by Nick Nolan & Danny Gill • **Master Class**
00695144 Book/CD Pack $17.99
00695910 DVD $19.95

Rock Lead Performance
by Nick Nolan & Danny Gill • **Master Class**
00695278 Book/CD Pack $17.95

Rock Lead Techniques
by Nick Nolan & Danny Gill • **Master Class**
00695146 Book/CD Pack $15.95

Slap & Pop Technique for Guitar
00695645 Book/CD Pack $14.99

Technique Exercises for Guitar
by Jean Marc Belkadi • **Private Lessons**
00695913 . . . . $14.95

Texas Blues Guitar
by Robert Calva • **Private Lessons**
00695340 Book/CD Pack $17.95

Ultimate Guitar Technique
by Bill LaFleur • **Private Lessons**
00695863 . . . . $19.95

BASS RECORDED VERSIONS

Bass Recorded Versions® feature authentic transcriptions written in standard notation and tablature for bass guitar. This series features complete bass lines from the classics to contemporary superstars.

25 All-Time Rock Bass Classics
00690445 / $14.95

25 Essential Rock Bass Classics
00690210 / $15.95

Aerosmith Bass Collection
00690413 / $17.95

Best of Victor Bailey
00690718 / $19.95

Bass Tab 1990-1999
00690400 / $16.95

Bass Tab 1999-2000
00690404 / $14.95

Bass Tab White Pages
00690508 / $29.95

The Beatles Bass Lines
00690170 / $14.95

The Beatles 1962-1966
00690556 / $18.99

The Beatles 1967-1970
00690557 / $18.99

Best Bass Rock Hits
00694803 / $12.95

**Black Sabbath –
We Sold Our Soul For Rock 'N' Roll**
00660116 / $17.95

The Best of Blink 182
00690549 / $18.95

Blues Bass Classics
00690291 / $14.95

Boston Bass Collection
00690935 / $19.95

Chart Hits for Bass
00690729 / $14.95

The Best of Eric Clapton
00660187 / $19.95

Stanley Clarke Collection
00672307 / $19.95

Funk Bass Bible
00690744 / $19.95

Hard Rock Bass Bible
00690746 / $17.95

**Jimi Hendrix –
Are You Experienced?**
00690371 / $17.95

The Buddy Holly Bass Book
00660132 / $12.95

Incubus – Morning View
00690639 / $17.95

Iron Maiden Bass Anthology
00690867 / $22.99

Best of Kiss for Bass
00690080 / $19.95

Bob Marley Bass Collection
00690568 / $19.95

Best of Marcus Miller
00690811 / $19.99

Motown Bass Classics
00690253 / $14.95

Mudvayne – Lost & Found
00690798 / $19.95

Nirvana Bass Collection
00690066 / $19.95

No Doubt – Tragic Kingdom
00120112 / $22.95

The Offspring – Greatest Hits
00690809 / $17.95

**Jaco Pastorius –
Greatest Jazz Fusion Bass Player**
00690421 / $17.95

The Essential Jaco Pastorius
00690420 / $18.95

Pearl Jam – Ten
00694882 / $14.95

Pink Floyd – Dark Side of the Moon
00660172 / $14.95

The Best of Police
00660207 / $14.95

Pop/Rock Bass Bible
00690747 / $17.95

Queen – The Bass Collection
00690065 / $17.95

R&B Bass Bible
00690745 / $17.95

Rage Against the Machine
00690248 / $16.95

The Best of Red Hot Chili Peppers
00695285 / $24.95

**Red Hot Chili Peppers –
Blood Sugar Sex Magik**
00690064 / $19.95

**Red Hot Chili Peppers –
By the Way**
00690585 / $19.95

**Red Hot Chili Peppers –
Californication**
00690390 / $19.95

**Red Hot Chili Peppers –
Greatest Hits**
00690675 / $18.95

**Red Hot Chili Peppers –
One Hot Minute**
00690091 / $18.95

**Red Hot Chili Peppers –
Stadium Arcadium**
00690853 / $24.95

**Red Hot Chili Peppers –
Stadium Arcadium: Deluxe Edition**
Book/2-CD Pack
00690863 / $39.95

Rock Bass Bible
00690446 / $19.95

Rolling Stones
00690256 / $16.95

System of a Down – Toxicity
00690592 / $19.95

Top Hits for Bass
00690677 / $14.95

**Stevie Ray Vaughan –
Lightnin' Blues 1983-1987**
00694778 / $19.95

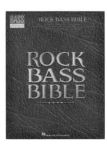

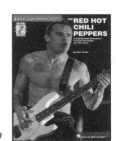

FOR MORE INFORMATION, SEE YOUR LOCAL MUSIC DEALER,
OR WRITE TO:

HAL•LEONARD® CORPORATION
7777 W. BLUEMOUND RD. P.O. BOX 13819 MILWAUKEE, WI 53213

Visit Hal Leonard Online at
www.halleonard.com

Prices, contents & availability subject to change without notice.
Some products may not be available outside the U.S.A.

0309

HAL·LEONARD BASS PLAY-ALONG

The Bass Play-Along Series will help you play your favorite songs quickly and easily! Just follow the tab, listen to the CD to hear how the bass should sound, and then play along using the separate backing tracks. The melody and lyrics are also included in the book in case you want to sing, or to simply help you follow along. The CD is enhanced so you can use your computer to adjust the recording to any tempo without changing pitch!

1. Rock
Songs: Another One Bites the Dust • Badge • Brown Eyed Girl • Come Together • The Joker • Low Rider • Money • Sweet Emotion.
00699674 Book/CD Pack............... $12.95

2. R&B
Songs: Get Ready • I Can't Help Myself (Sugar Pie, Honey Bunch) • I Got You (I Feel Good) • I Heard It Through the Grapevine • I Want You Back • In the Midnight Hour • My Girl • You Can't Hurry Love.
00699675 Book/CD Pack............... $12.95

3. Pop/Rock
Songs: Crazy Little Thing Called Love • Crocodile Rock • Maneater • My Life • No Reply at All • Peg • Message in a Bottle • Suffragette City.
00699677 Book/CD Pack............... $12.95

4. '90s Rock
Songs: All I Wanna Do • Fly Away • Give It Away • Hard to Handle • Jeremy • Know Your Enemy • Spiderwebs • You Oughta Know.
00699679 Book/CD Pack............... $12.95

5. Funk
Songs: Brick House • Cissy Strut • Get Off • Get Up (I Feel Like Being) a Sex Machine • Higher Ground • Le Freak • Pick up the Pieces • Super Freak.
00699680 Book/CD Pack............... $12.95

6. Classic Rock
Songs: Free Ride • Funk #49 • Gimme Three Steps • Green-Eyed Lady • Radar Love • Werewolves of London • White Room • Won't Get Fooled Again.
00699678 Book/CD Pack............... $12.95

7. Hard Rock
Songs: Crazy Train • Detroit Rock City • Iron Man • Livin' on a Prayer • Living After Midnight • Peace Sells • Smoke on the Water • The Trooper.
00699676 Book/CD Pack............... $14.95

8. Punk Rock
Songs: Brain Stew • Buddy Holly • Dirty Little Secret • Fat Lip • Flavor of the Weak • Gotta Get Away • Lifestyles of the Rich and Famous • Man Overboard.
00699813 Book/CD Pack............... $12.95

9. Blues
Songs: All Your Love (I Miss Loving) • Born Under a Bad Sign • I'm Tore Down • I'm Your Hoochie Coochie Man • Killing Floor • Pride and Joy • Sweet Home Chicago • The Thrill Is Gone.
00699817 Book/CD Pack............... $12.95

10. Jimi Hendrix Smash Hits
Songs: All Along the Watchtower • Can You See Me? • Crosstown Traffic • Fire • Foxey Lady • Hey Joe • Manic Depression • Purple Haze • Red House • Remember • Stone Free • The Wind Cries Mary.
00699815 Book/CD Pack............... $16.95

11. Country
Songs: Achy Breaky Heart (Don't Tell My Heart) • All My Ex's Live in Texas • Boot Scootin' Boogie • Chattahoochee • Guitars, Cadillacs • I Like It, I Love It • Should've Been a Cowboy • T-R-O-U-B-L-E.
00699818 Book/CD Pack............... $12.95

13. Lennon & McCartney
Songs: All My Loving • Back in the U.S.S.R. • Day Tripper • Eight Days a Week • Get Back • I Saw Her Standing There • Nowhere Man • Paperback Writer.
00699816 .... $14.99

21. Rock Band – Modern Rock
Songs: Are You Gonna Be My Girl • Black Hole Sun • Creep • Dani California • In Bloom • Learn to Fly • Say It Ain't So • When You Were Young.
00700705 Book/CD Pack............... $14.95

22. Rock Band – Classic Rock
Songs: Ballroom Blitz • Detroit Rock City • Don't Fear the Reaper • Gimme Shelter • Highway Star • Mississippi Queen • Suffragette City • Train Kept A-Rollin'.
00700706 Book/CD Pack............... $14.95

23. Pink Floyd – Dark Side of The Moon
Songs: Any Colour You Like • Brain Damage • Breathe • Eclipse • Money • Time • Us and Them.
00700847 Book/CD Pack............... $14.99

FOR MORE INFORMATION,
SEE YOUR LOCAL MUSIC DEALER,
OR WRITE TO:

HAL·LEONARD®
CORPORATION
7777 W. BLUEMOUND RD. P.O. BOX 13819
MILWAUKEE, WISCONSIN 53213

Visit Hal Leonard Online at **www.halleonard.com**

Prices, contents, and availability subject to change without notice.

0409